Life in Scotland

Rosalind Mitchison

Life in
Scotland

'The true state of every nation is the
state of common life.'

Samuel Johnson

B. T. BATSFORD LTD, London

To my mother

First published 1978

© Rosalind Mitchison 1978

Printed and bound in Great Britain
by Weatherby Woolnough, Wellingborough, Northants

for the publishers B. T. Batsford Ltd,
4 Fitzhardinge Street, London W1H 0AH

ISBN 0 7134 1559 2

Contents

List of illustrations

Acknowledgements

No student of Scottish history can work without a deep sense of obligation to the two great archives, the Scottish Record Office and the National Library of Scotland. The help that has been received from the staff of these institutions goes far beyond what anyone has a right to expect, and is infused with scholarship, courtesy and kindness. I also wish to record my recognition of the stimulus to thought and research that comes from all levels of the University community in Edinburgh, and in particular my debt to my colleague, Professor T. C. Smout, whose *History of the Scottish People* will long remain a major element in our understanding of the past. Finally, this book is offered to the person who has most constantly and for the longest period of time shown me the fascination of history.

The author and publishers would like to thank Marion Berman for her picture research and the following for permission to reproduce illustrations: fig.37 is reproduced by Gracious Permission of H.M. the Queen; the Earl of Ancaster (fig.14); the Duke of Atholl (fig.16); the British Library (figs. 1 & 5); photo Camera Press (fig.38); Campbeltown Public Library (figs. 15 & 30); Edinburgh University Library, G. W. Wilson Collection (fig.3); photo A. F. Kersting (figs. 23 & 24); photo Morrison, McChlery & Co., Glasgow (fig.12); National Galleries of Scotland (figs. 6, 13, 17 & 18); National Museum of Antiquities of Scotland (fig.4); photo National Trust for Scotland (figs. 21 & 22); the National Coal Board (fig.36); Radio Times Hulton Picture Library (figs. 8-11 and pages 51 & 120); Royal Commission on Ancient Monuments, Scotland (figs. 34a & b); Scottish Country Life Museum (fig.28); Smith's Institute, Stirling - photo National Monuments Record of Scotland (fig.2); photo Eileen Tweedy (figs. 26, 29 & 33); University of St Andrews (fig.7). The remaining illustrations are from the publishers' collection.

SCOTLAND

0   50
MILES

0   80
KILOMETRES

ORKNEY

STROMA

CAITHNESS

SUTHERLAND

LEWIS

HARRIS

NORTH UIST

BERNERAY H.

BENBECULA

SOUTH UIST

ROSS & CROMARTY

MORAY

BANFF

SKYE

RAASAY

Inverness

ABERDEEN

Aberdeen

BARRA

SANDRAY

PABBAY

BERNERAY

CANNA

EIGG

MUCK

INVERNESS

HIGHLANDS

COLL

NORTH ARGYLL

TIREE

LORN

IONA

MULL

PERTH

Dundee

COLONSAY

MID-ARGYLL

FIFE

COWAL

Stirling

STIRLING

ISLAY

KNAPDALE

LOTHIAN

Edinburgh

Glasgow

ARRAN

BERWICK

KINTYRE

PEEBLES

LOWLANDS

ROXBURGH

DUMFRIES

WIGTOWN

KIRKCUDBRIGHT

— Chapter 1 —

Scotland before the Reformation

'The stait of man dois change et vary
Now sound, now seik, now blyth, now sary
Now dansand mirry, now like to dee;
Timor Mortis Conturbat me.'

Dunbar

T HIS is a book of social history. This means that its two main concerns are the structure of society and the material conditions of life for the different groups within that society. These two aspects, structure and standards of living, tie social history on the one hand to constitutional history and on the other to economic history. They also interact. The kinds of structure a society can have are limited by the nature of its economy: the material conditions of life for everyone depend on the personal rights that a society's structure allows and protects. Sooner or later in looking at a society we have to go on the one hand to law, religion and tradition, on the other to geography and climate.

Let us start with the basic facts of geography and climate. Scotland is a northern country with a wet, windy and unstable climate singularly unsuited for growing the basic cereal crops of early European agriculture. Modern Scotland, which has some of the most skilled and productive farming of the world, disguises this fact to the observer. The land drainers of the nineteenth century ended the problem of sour, waterlogged soil, at least in lowland areas. The wider range of crops brought in in the eighteenth century and the improved strains of the twentieth have also done much to insulate the countryside from the vagaries of the weather. But in the sixteenth and seventeenth centuries men had neither the knowledge nor the resources to make secure their agricultural livelihood, and for undeveloped countries agriculture is the main source of livelihood. Soaked land came late to seed-time and dangerously late to harvest. We can see from notes in the kirk session register of Elgin, in the temperate clime of Morayshire, recording the peals of bells in thanksgiving of harvest, that October was the normal harvest month,[1] but in Scotland frost can easily strike in September. Every few years winter would arrive before the harvest was secured. Even if this did not happen, farming was inefficient. Seed yielded a low return, and this perpetuated itself, for the large ration of product that had to be reserved as seed, often a third, meant that farmers kept the worst for this purpose. Cattle were often underfed, half-starved in winter, and did not breed well. All this meant what we would think of as grinding poverty for most people, and insecurity as well.

Scotland is not only a northerly country, she is one where communications are difficult. Great arms of the sea, firths or sea lochs, stretch into the land. Hills in the south and mountains in the north dictate not only the possible routes of roads but curtail the area of farmland. The coastal plain, though fertile, is sometimes merely a narrow strip. The hills and inlets made difficulties for trade. More basically they made difficulties for government. They hindered the

12

growth of a merchant class, that element in primitive societies most concerned to preserve peace and the rule of law, and they gave additional reasons, if such were needed, why the orders of the central government could often be disregarded. For to this initial geographical obstacle to strong government had been added the devastating and demoralising effect of the long wars of independence with England, and the unfortunate accident of a series of royal minorities in the fifteenth and sixteenth centuries. In these 200 years no monarch succeeded as an adult. During the long periods of regal infancy the country did not sink into total anarchy but the general slackening of central power meant that each monarch, once grown up, had to start where his father had done, regain the elements of government power from the noble families that had usurped them, and restart the concept of the rule of law. For long periods, as Acts of Parliament would announce, the king's lieges had not been 'servit of the law'.

Scotland was, by derivation, very much a Celtic country. In the eleventh century she had been almost completely Gaelic speaking. Her monarchy, her law, her culture then were predominantly those that the invading Scots had brought from Ireland. Since then she had been subject to other important influences, to Norman governing institutions, to an English urban element and the English language, to close ties of King and nobility with Anglo-Norman society, to French soldiers and the French language, and to renewed contacts with Scandinavia by trade. But some of the basic features of Celtic society remained. In the sixteenth century the north-west and west, the Highlands and the Western Isles, were entirely Gaelic speaking and with a Gaelic culture. Music, poetry and social structure were as in Ireland. Elsewhere in many ways the Anglo-Saxon speech typified the dominance of Anglo-Saxon culture. But through the whole of Scottish society one basic feature still showed her Celtic element, the structure of kinship. Kinship, cousinship, the ties of a common surname held men together by a bond that was so taken for granted that it is difficult to get a clear impression of its importance. In the Highlands kinship, real or imagined, was the basis of the dominant political unit, the clan, with its head the chief; though even here feudal overlordship, introduced by Scottish kings, provided an alternative network of obligation and relationship, less compelling but still important. The situation was not far different in the Borders, where the border surnames, often allied to a feudal relationship, held together large bodies of men; but here the culture, predominantly Anglo-Saxon, gave border society a more explicit emphasis on the role of feudal lordship. Here also the lesser distance of the Borders from the central government deprived it of the near immunity from the king's

striking power enjoyed by Highland society. Kings could, and did
persistently, carry raids into the Borders to put into action their own
concept of law and order, and to extract pledges of good behaviour
which would, for a while, override the obligations of existing feuds
and rivalries. Even so, the power and ambitions of the head of a border
family, such as the Scotts, the Homes, or one or other of the branches
of the Kers, was different not in kind but only in degree from that of a
chief of Clan Cameron or the head of a branch of the MacDonalds.

Kinship in Scotland could involve the recognition of distant links,
but its base was one-sided. It encouraged local cohesiveness.
Landowners would install their own kin as tenants on their land,
and the acknowledged relationship was the best security such
tenure could have. They would so build up a local society in
which kinship and lordship mutually supported each other and
together promoted peace and order. Where natural boundaries
coincided with the areas under occupation by one surname and its
dependencies, the system of kinship was a force for peace. But in
the wider issues of national peace the system encouraged separation
and feud unless it was drastically modified or curtailed by other
bonds.

Scottish kinship, as recent work has shown, was an exclusively
patrilineal affair.[2] The surname, because it came from the father's
side, was the crucial link in the chains of society. Intermarriage
between surnames, though perhaps blocked in particular instances
by traditions of separation, was usually made easy by the inadequacy of links on the female side. The cognate bond did not hold
men and their policies together. Where society was at its most
brutal, as in highland and border warfare, men would readily attack
and kill their near relatives on the female side in the course of well-
established feuds[3] and sixteenth century methods of warfare, which
included burning down towers, churches and other refuges, meant
that women and children were also at risk. Because of this one-sided
attitude to kinship the pacifying effect of the acknowledgment of
kin in a small area did little to advance peace on the wider scale.

All status in society has links with matters of the past; even where
status is simply determined by skills, these are the results of past
training. But a kinship-based society is bound to status almost totally
determined in the past, and in the distant past too, in most cases. It
is likely, therefore, to be socially very conservative. The function of
the main manifestation of its culture, the bard or poet, is often to
recount genealogy. Poet and bard, piper, councillor, arms bearer,
and other officials of a clan were often born to hereditary office. In
highland society these posts were usually possessed by sub-groups

within the clan, bearing a different surname, and this system of offices gave a link holding together separate kins in a wider society. The existence of specialized, hereditary callings was in no way unusual in the sixteenth century. Craftsmen, noblemen, peasants and merchants were all exercising hereditary functions. But it was by then unusual to have hereditary designation for what we today think of as intellectual or artistic activities—the decline of the hereditary professorships of some Italian universities, for instance, had come about because of the difficulty of breeding men possessed of the right abilities and interests. The survival of such hereditary posts in highland society is a mark of its lack of adaptability. A kinship society will have a multitude of gradations, separated by fine but inexorable lines, in a way that is different from the broad, modern separations of class. It will be a status-dominated society with the key to that status, family, lying in the past. Not for nothing did most highland clans use as surname some filial derivative. A man's lineage was what mattered most to him. This kind of society does not prevent communication between the different levels. The unchangeable nature of its hierarchy means that no defences of status are necessary. Celtic society has long had, therefore, a freedom of speech across class or status barriers, relatively lacking, for instance, in Anglo-Saxon society. But unless modified by other institutions it has had a lack of mobility, in both social and geographic terms. This lack of mobility was enhanced by the ineffectiveness of marriage links, since in other societies marriage has tended to be an important mechanism in movement up or down the social scale.

The most authoritative recent work on Scottish social history sums up the basic social structure of early Scotland thus: 'Highland society was based on kinship modified by feudalism, lowland society on feudalism tempered by kinship. Both systems were aristocratic, unconscious of class, designed for war'.[4] In the sixteenth century in the Lowlands kinship was in decline. Less and less was it the leading element in men's imagination. This is shown in the anecdotes and minor events collected by Chambers in his *Domestic Annals* where it is clear that the imagination and sympathy of society went out towards events involving the nobility and gentry in a way it did not to lesser folk.[5] In the stories of crime, violence, bereavement or seduction, it is the reaction of those gently born that holds the interest of the raconteur. Some of the appeal of lordship was based on the same interests as make the private lives of film stars news in the twentieth century. Lordship had other strengths. Originally feudal lordship had been brought in by the king as an

institution which defined and strengthened his rights. It was
imposed on the standard type of rural society in western Europe, a
peasantry farming the land and an aristocracy with military, political
and organising functions, receiving rents and goods from the
peasants. It tightened and defined this structure. The overlord was
the king's vassal and through him would come military support to
the king and justice and defence to the peasantry. Such at any rate
was the theory. In practice with the king lacking his own military
resources, lordship was not always a source of peace or protection to
the peasantry. The nobles had often taken advantage of royal
minorities or royal preoccupations to subject the country to their
feuds and rivalries. Their own loyalty lay first to the interests of
their own house or name, and lordship was a means of exalting
these, of widening the kinship group over which their influence
lay, to include men not allied by blood. The more peaceful methods
of doing this had been by a peculiar Scottish institution, the bond of
manrent, a written commitment that could be made by men of
adherence to a particular great lord. Cruder methods were irascibly
described by James VI at the of the sixteenth century in his
comments on the nobility in his *Basilicon Doron*:

> Their honor stood in committing three points of iniquity: to thrall,
> by oppression, the meaner sort that dwelleth neere them . . . to
> maintaine their servants and dependers in any wrong . . . and . . .
> to bang it out bravelie, he and all his kinne, against him and all his
> . . .[6]

The Scottish aristocracy showed all the greed for power found in
the dominant groups in undeveloped nations where the central
government is weak. They had no objection to material riches, but
power was more important to them. In any case they and the
monarch took for granted a high standard of material things. They
assumed that the main possessions and pleasures owned by the
aristocracy of richer realms in Europe should be theirs too: wine to
drink, furs and fine fabrics to wear, armour, horses, castles and
weapons suited to a military way of life (for the aristocracy still had
a real military function), equipment for the sports of hawking and
hunting, and a certain amount of domestic luxury, silver plate,
furniture and hangings. The rents of the peasantry, normally paid in
grain, would be sold to give purchasing power for these items of
equipment. If income fell short of supplying this way of life, the
most obvious ways to increase it were at the expense of good
government. One way had been to browbeat the central administration and extract a share of its revenue. Hijacking the customs
receipts was a favourite form of this. Another was to enlarge the

landed base, either by marrying an heiress or by grabbing the territory of another house. Both could involve open or concealed coercion. Political pressure on the crown could be used to legalize such aggrandizement. But increasingly, as the costs of what king and nobility and great churchmen regarded as necessities of life — mostly objects that had to be bought abroad — rose more quickly than the value of rents, they had turned to a new way of raising revenue. This was the institution of feu ferm. By this land was granted out in perpetuity in return for a cash payment and a subsequent fixed rent in money. This practice had spread particularly widely in the fifteenth century and created a new and important class of tenants who were almost owners of their land, secure and, with successive depreciations of money, increasingly prosperous. These were the lairds, the 'baronage of Scotland' as they were called.

The rise of the class of lairds gradually transformed society. It meant that the head of a surname had men securely holding land under him who might or might not be part of his kin. Feus tended to go to the strongest and richest bidders rather than to relatives. These men would be under the noble's lordship, and their existence is part of the development in lowland society of lordship at the expense of kinship. In fact the very action of creating feu ferm was often at the expense of many of those whose claim on the great noble had been solely that of kin. These men had been known as 'kindly tenants', a phrase that implies not a generous or friendly relationship but one based on the claim of kin. It was, in many cases, not clearly defined nor secure, since kinship had been a stronger security than legal definition. It rested on the assumption that all men would stand by their kin. When feus were available some kindly tenants would win them, and eventually provide families for the class of lairds at the poorer end, the bonnet lairds of the seventeenth century, men who farmed their own land with small pretensions to rank but with security of tenure. Those kindly tenants who failed to obtain these prizes might lose their lands altogether. Kin was no longer sufficient security. If they failed, they would be forced down the social and economic scale. A lord who valued money above kin would raise their rents. They might become sub-tenants under their rivals. In any case their security had gone.

So the rise of feu ferm, though a force for law and order in that it established permanent rights in land, did not benefit the peasantry. Security of tenure in most cases stopped at the class of lairds. Kindly tenants gradually became indistinguishable from tenants at will, and mixed with the general run of small peasants. Unlike the neighbour-

ing countries of France and England, in Scotland the peasant,
though personally free, had no fixed legal rights in the soil he tilled,
and usually no agreement with his lord that gave him any definite
period of security. Major describes the tenants in the fifteenth
century as holding 'at the pleasure of the lord of the soil' and draws
the obvious picture of the results of this: 'they do not dare to build
good houses though stone abound; neither do they plant trees or
hedges for their orchards, nor do they dung the land'; he summed
the situation up as 'no small loss and damage to the whole realm.'[7]
Peasant security does not need to be legally confirmed to exist. It
can be based on accepted common interests with the landlord, or
backed by specialist techniques which make an individual peasant
irreplaceable. In Scotland neither of these aids existed in the
sixteenth or seventeenth centuries, and insecurity; by encouraging
bad farming, was an important source of rural poverty.

The more powerful and prosperous of the lairds formed the group
known as the baronage, holding their lands either by tenancy in
chief or as sub-tenants of the aristocracy. Their 'baronies' entitled
them to a baron court. This was a place for minor criminal matters,
though in the Highlands, where the power of the king's courts did
not obtain, a petty chief could exercise capital punishment. It also
made possible the system of joint farming, settling questions of
boundaries, straying animals, damage by one peasant to the
property of another. It was a place where debts could be enforced,
and in particular where the laird could insist on payment of rents
and labour services due to him. The court might also enforce Acts of
Parliament. A barony would include several joint farms, held by a
group of tenants and farmed partly by joint efforts, and always in
holdings that lay mixed together. The joint farm, and the farm-town
where the peasantry lived, was not a permanent unit. Tenants
would change as the years passed. But it was the basic social unit of
Scottish rural life outside the family: four, six or eight households
living in fairly close proximity and carrying on some enterprises
together, all closely affected by the actions of each other. In most
parts of Scotland there were not the large nuclear villages found in
lowland areas of Europe — whether spread along a street, as often in
England or northern France, or clustered round a church as in the
Low Countries or southern France.[8] She tended therefore to lack the
specialist workers and the markets that can be so important in rural
standards of living. Markets, anyway, were a privileged possession,
still confined to a narrow list of towns. A barony would have its
smith, wright and miller, but often few other skilled tradesmen, no
cobblers or bakers, for instance. Smiths sometimes, millers always,

were supported by payments in grain from the peasantry. Probably in the case of the smith these payments were not resented. Iron and iron equipment were obvious necessities of life and payment was for value appreciated. But millers, as local businessmen, and their dues, were everywhere resented. The peasants were bound by thirlage to take their corn to specified mills, and as the mill was the most expensive piece of rural investment, the laird expected a good rent for it which would not come in if it was not used. In many cases he extracted a proportional payment of the corn ground, and in all cases the miller and his assistant did so, so that the total burden could be heavy — over ten per cent of the grain. There could be delays, particularly in dry seasons when the streams would not work the wheel of a mill, and there was always room for suspicion of theft or adulteration. Security, convenience and economy were all reasons for keeping an illegal hand quern. General resentment of thirlage and the miller gave unity to men in a barony, Otherwise, because of the scattered farm structure, if anything made a barony into a community it was the occasional meetings of its court. In this court there was a part for the peasantry to play, as birlaymen or jury and living witness of the custom of the barony.

For all this it seems unlikely that the barony was a social unit likely to arouse loyalty. Even seeing this at its most positive, in the records of such courts, one is aware that a large part of its time was spent in police duties, and another section in enforcing the claims of the laird. Lordship was gradually replacing kinship as the dominant social link in the Lowlands, but in doing so it was failing to be a full replacement. The gap was not immediately obvious. So long as Scottish society was subject to internal disturbances, private or local wars and political issues that raised local sectional adherence, the military function of the nobility still carried weight. It was possible to think of the baronage and nobility as defending their tenantry. This was not a really valid concept, for even by the fifteenth century the castles of Scotland were obviously built to hold only the household of the castellan and his soldiers, not to be a refuge for the local population. In the sixteenth century the upper classes still occupied castles or fortified houses. These might be very elaborate, as befitted a social group that took its own safety seriously. Craignethan in Lanarkshire, the fortress of James V's favourite, Hamilton of Finnart, later to be the model for Tillietudlem in Scott's *Old Mortality*, has recently been shown to have had the first *caponnier* in Britain. This was the latest defensive device of the mid-sixteenth century, and was till lately thought of as almost exclusively Italian. The lords and lairds of sixteenth-century Scotland still monopolized the attention of government and society, but as, after the middle years of the century, English invasion ceased to be a serious risk, their military activities cannot be seen as of benefit to their tenantry at large. The tie of lordship contained less of mutual benefit than did the tie of kinship that it had superseded. As this process went on there was therefore a tendency for society to lack a sense of unity and joint purpose to hold it together.

It might be expected that the church would fill this gap. The Catholic church was a body to which all men owed allegiance. They had become members of it as infants, and either lived by its rules or accepted them as valid, adhered to its dogma and eschatology and died aided by its rites. The church provided the units of time out of which life was built, the pattern of six days work followed by rest, worship and ceremony on Sunday, the seasons of the Christian year in which the life of Christ and the early church was relived, and, most important, overlaying the weekly pattern, the fasts and festivals. It also provided a host of specialized careers, available either for those of unusual ability, or, more often, those with the right family connections.

By the early sixteenth century the Catholic church did not provide much more than this. The great bulk of parishes were starved of revenue in favour of other institutions: monasteries, cathedral chapters and universities. The parish priest had little time and no incentive to be much more than a farmer of his glebe. He could not instruct his flock and his literacy in Latin was barely enough for the performance of his liturgical function. And in the late fifteenth century there had set in a decline of the specialized institutions which had mopped up the wealth of the church. The nobility started to plunder the church, not in the crude, physical way in which they had sometimes done so in the past, by pillage and destruction, but by the more refined and more totally devastating technique of using it to support their families. The kings joined in this too, placing illegitimate children in important posts. As a result the bishoprics became part of the property of the great families, and the discipline of the monasteries crumbled as more and more of the abbots were non-resident, under age and, effectively, laymen. The effect on the monasteries was particularly disastrous. The monastic life needs a sense of special challenge, and a cenobitic house needs leadership: neither was forthcoming, so that discipline and devotion, already rare, were extinguished. In the secular church the effect was less total. History abounds with instances of good professional work being done by people appointed for the wrong reasons, or by people desperately short of the materials they need for their work. But cumulatively the effect was that the church had by 1550 ceased to be an institution effectively presenting the image of a spiritual life to the mass of the laity, or receiving participation and loyalty from laymen.

Monsignor McRoberts has recently shown us in articles in the *Innes Review*[9] the picture of a cathedral canon in Glasgow living in what were then very comfortable conditions. His mistress, children and servants shared with him a house of several rooms, and he owned many fine things, a fur-lined cloak, jewellery and plate. His household was more luxurious than would be found among the laity, except for the richest and greatest of merchants or nobles. He may have functioned as a money lender. The way of life of such a man included a ritual element of mass-saying that did not belong to the laity, but otherwise involved no element of self-denial, sanctity or religious experience that could justify the possession of special privileges, and would be a handicap to the church if it had to defend its position.

In this picture of a society lacking strong, coherent bonds, whether of a secular or religious kind, one area stands out as an exception, the life of the towns. The burghs of Scotland in the sixteenth century were mostly not yet examples of what we would consider urban life. Burgesses still often grazed cattle on the town's lands and might raise crops too. The 'neat herd' was a necessary servant of the burgh. The towns, as an English observer was to remark as late as 1650, deserved no other appellation than village in most cases.[10] Even so, this urban element was economically important to the country. Through the royal burghs flowed the thin but important stream of foreign trade, while the lesser burghs provided the inadequate markets for rural life, and crude industries such as of cloth and leather. Trade was thought of as a privilege and a possession. Like other forms of possession the right to it was specific, usually obtained by birth or marriage. The position of craftsmen in the town was also hereditary. There was not much shift of people between town and country. Recruitment into the towns, made necessary by the higher risks of disease there, had little effect on the countryside. The towns were a small privileged enclave in the kingdom, and the way of life of a merchant in a Scottish seaport was probably nearer to that of his counterpart and associates in Copenhagen or Campveere, whom he would meet on his voyages, than to that of his rural compatriots. But the towns were one type of institution that made a real call on the activity and loyalty of the citizen.

Scottish burghs were the scene of a long struggle in the fifteenth and sixteenth centuries between the merchants and craftsmen for dominance in government. On the whole the merchants won, but the craftsmen retained a proportion of places on the council. Each group had its own gild, and in some places the craftsmen had more than one. In Ayr the basic distinction within the crafts was between the 'hammermen' and those whose techniques used muscle power less noisily. Gilds carried on their own social life, and so did the burgh as a whole. Two consecutive entries in the Edinburgh treasurer's accounts for Christmas 1554 remind us that town life had its own organized entertainments:

> Six shillings and eightpence for 'beiring of daillis, greit treis, and punshionis to ma ane skaffald in the Tolbuith to play the Clerk Play on, and away bringing of it agane'. Eightpence for 'towis to bind the twa men that slew George Dromond, quhen thai wer hedit'.[11]

The frequency of executions and other physical punishments at the orders of burgh councils not only reminds us of the violence and cruelty of life at this time, but reveals the forceful and vivid authority that these councils exercised over townsmen. Burghs kept the peace, fixed the prices and conditions of sale and attempted rudimentary control over epidemics, all with draconian penalties. It is not surprising that the religious revolution of the Reformation should have particularly relied on the activity and enthusiasms of the urban population in a way not explained by the few thousand it numbered.

Townsmen were, of course, in close contact with foreign cities. A merchant in the sixteenth century travelled with his goods, and knew foreign streets and quays as well as he knew his own. There would be members of his family abroad for many years on end, acting either as agent or learning the business and making contacts as young men in other firms. There were other types of foreign contact. Scholars went abroad to foreign universities and moved about in an international academic world which was to be broken up by Reformation and Counter-Reformation, not to re-form until the twentieth century. A steady stream of routine ecclesiastical business went from Scotland to Rome. Monasteries might have links with houses abroad: there was for instance a Scottish house at Ratisbon. Scottish noblemen had been in the habit of earning their livings as leaders of mercenary troops abroad, and sometimes received foreign estates to add to their ones at home. In the early sixteenth century the Duke of Albany, Regent of Scotland, had come from France to govern the country without any language at his command except

French. It is a commonplace that Scots speech still uses words that have come from the French. These are usually for the minor amenities or civilities of life, a reminder of the difference in cultural levels between the two countries. The most extreme example, the warning cry of 'Gardy loo' in Edinburgh in the eighteenth century, suggests that of all the people coming to Scotland it was only the French who were so fastidious as to object to having what we today call 'untreated sewage' thrown on them from above. There were so many Scottish people in Scandinavia that the word 'Schotts' became synonymous there with small trader. Foreign influence — and we must remember that for all the similarities of speech England was as foreign as France — brought the Reformation to Scotland, with effects to be seen in the next chapter. It also brought most of the elements of gracious living of sixteenth- and seventeenth-century Scotland, and many of the styles in which these were expressed, from the tall Dutch gables of the houses in the little ports of Fife to the elegant scenes in the Books of Hours used by the royal family.

Most of sixteenth-century Scotland lived without much graciousness, in houses of one room, earth-floored, walled by stone or turf, roofed with turf and usually without a chimney. The Lowlands were already severely deforested. Wood for building had to be imported, and was expensive. So the use of good timber would be confined to the couples at each end of the room, the door and perhaps a wood-panelled window. In such a house cleanliness, comfort, decency and careful preparation of food would be almost impossible. Contemporaries do not directly tell us about the way of life of humble people, so we have to get our glimpses of it from minor and occasional items. We know that in Edinburgh the council chamber had glass in its windows in the mid-sixteenth century, but also that many houses, even those directly on the High Street, did not as late as the 1630s. There was very little privacy at any point on the social scale. It was impossible for those who lived in one-roomed cottages. It is possible that families often shared houses. In 1624 a devastating fire in Dunfermline is on record as destroying 120 houses and leaving 287 families homeless.[12] The corridor, the architectural innovation that enables people to treat a room as private, arrived in Scotland only in the late seventeenth century, and then only for the upper class. Queen, aristocracy and great lairds in the sixteenth century lived in crowded and cramped circumstances, and when a laird or nobleman had a house in Edinburgh it would consist of five or six rooms only, for family and servants. Status and comfort came much more from the ability to command services than goods. A man of substance rode abroad with many underlings, as much for safety as for prestige. We have a picture of a highland chief 'visiting' in the 1580s with 86 followers, and the Master of Yester in East Lothian, going about with 48.[13] The pleasures of the rich, such as hunting, fine clothes, and where attainable, personal cleanliness, all involved a great many attendants, and the inefficient farming of the day was also prodigal of labour. This was not only a charge on the economy. It was a sign of the fact that the value placed by society on the time and lives of the lower orders was slight.

— Chapter 2 —

The Revolutions of the Sixteenth Century

'Smalaidh mis an tuha
Mar a smaladh Muire
Comraig Bhride's Mhuire
Air an tula's air an lar
'S air an fhardaich uile.'

'I will smoor the hearth
As Mary would smoor;
The encompassment of Bride
    and of Mary
On the fire and on the floor
And on the household all.'

Gaelic song for smooring the fire

T HE slow changes of early society, the decay of the bond of kinship, the spreading corruption within the church, the slow accumulation of wealth, give way to rapid change in the economic, religious and political revolutions of the sixteenth century. In 1560 Calvinism became the only legally accepted and permitted form of religion in Scotland and in 1567 a baronial revolution confirmed this settlement. The religious revolution went through very simply. There was some inefficient fighting, mostly by foreign troops, English and French, on the two sides. Neither Catholics nor Protestants made martyrs in any quantity. The baronial revolution may have seemed a more serious event. It involved some prolonged and bitter fighting, as well as assassinations and executions. In the event its effect was transitory for as the puppet king of the baronial faction the nobility installed the infant James VI, who grew up to be the first successful administrator of Scotland, the gradual imposer of a minimum level of law and order. In the last 22 years of his reign James ruled the country from England, partly by means of a new, professional aristocracy and partly by the professionalizing of the system of justice. Gradually lowland Scotland adopted new standards of law and order. The political revolution, as achieved in 1567, was gradually undone in favour of James's own great achievement. It was, therefore, in the long run, the religious revolution that really achieved a drastic break with the past; the imposition of a new church order directly, and, indirectly, of new ways of life and relationships between individuals.

In one way the religious revolution merely confirmed the existing system, the securing by the nobility of the goods of the church. At first it looked as if the nobility would retain the whole wealth of the church, both land and teind, on which it had already a powerful grip. The existing Catholic clergy were connected to the great families and could not be deprived of their revenues during their lifetimes, and afterwards the families would be difficult to dislodge. The new Protestant church put forward an ecclesiastical and social programme, *The Book of Discipline*, that would need money. There were to be ministers in every parish amply supported, superintendents above them, schools and universities to provide the educated laity and ministry, and relief for the poor. This would have made use of the entire revenue of the old church. The Protestant nobility had no intention of surrendering wealth on this scale. Eventually a compromise was reached, that a third of the revenues of benefices should be shared between the crown and the church, and on this uncertain basis of income the church began to create its parish ministry. The immediate problem was more one of man-power than of money. Gradually during the sixteenth century the church built up an educated ministry. If there was no-one available to be a qualified minister in a parish, a 'reader' or an 'exhorter' was installed. Most parishes in southern Scotland were served at some sort of level by 1570, and by a fully-fledged minister by 1590. In the north east the ministry was basically installed by 1600.[1] In the Highlands the whole process was much slower, even after parishes had been grouped together into bigger units, and many areas were left for two generations with little in the way of ministry. The question of property also took time, and the king's attempts to clarify and complete this process were a major source of the breach between him and his nobility which led to the Great Rebellion of the seventeenth century.

The spread of the Protestant ministry was the spread of the preaching of Calvinism, of the utter depravity of mankind, the uselessness of so-called good works, of salvation only by faith which proceeds 'from no natural powers within us' as the Confession of 1560 says, but is the inspiration of the Holy Ghost. God has selected some for salvation, and his spirit will take possession of their hearts and turn them to be of service. Others he has decided to leave in their natural darkness. The basic element of Calvinist dogma has always seemed to outsiders its determinism, the predestination of men either to salvation or damnation. No action of man can do anything to move an individual from one classification to the other, but to those 'elect' chosen for salvation, God will give some intimation of the fact. They will be 'assured', and their outward lives and conduct will show some element of this.

This might be expected to become an individualistic faith with no place for the kirk or for the sense of community. It might lead to the sloth of despair or self-satisfaction, or to aggressive self-righteousness. In fact it sometimes did. But in general the determinism of Calvin provided, as later did the determinism of Marx, a great force for action, for the reshaping of men's lives and institutions. That it did so was partly because Calvin's own thought was deeply informed with a sense of society and of the need to live in it, but also because the early reformers, particularly in Scotland, were imbued with morality. The language of the 1560 Confession of Faith (as later the language of the Communist manifesto) breathes the moral spirit that its argument at times denies. 'Works' may be no road to salvation, but a godly life and a godly society are the outward signs of the infusion of the Holy Ghost, of the acceptability of men to God. The elect fight against sin in daily life and in this fight are aided by Christ. The church is the society of God's chosen. Its structure must help the members to live godly lives, and also, since there is bound to be some mixture of the reprobate in any human society, censure and control the wicked. It is not for nothing that the blueprint of the new church, put out immediately after the 'Reformation' of 1560, has the title *The Book of Discipline*. It envisages a hierarchy of church governments, culminating in an ecclesiastical parliament for the whole country of laymen and clergy, a body which came to be known as the General Assembly.

By the end of the sixteenth century the structure of the church had gone a long way towards the plans of 1560. Below the General Assembly came the other courts, the synod, the presbytery and the kirk sessions. There was a vocal 'presbyterian' movement in the church which held that the presbytery, combining elders and ministers from a group of parishes, should be regarded as the essence of the church, and should rule without any superior, whether superintendent or bishop. There were difficulties in the way of this programme. One was the insistence by the king on the retention of some functions for bishops. Another was the practical problem of creating a real eldership in a backward society. Even where there were some parishioners able to read, as in the towns, the educating of the people in this form of self-government took some time.

For, in spite of the theory of presbyterianism, the essence of the new system lay in the government at the lowest level, the kirk session. This local committee ruled its parish like a modern cabinet. It met regularly, usually on a Sunday after church, but also as required. It investigated moral lapses. It enforced the new standards of Sunday observance which came in in the 1590s, seeing to it that everyone went to church on Sunday twice, and that 'between sermons' they did not engage in any frivolous activity. It raised and distributed funds for poor relief. Altogether it was a remarkable institution. It was not supposed to carry the whole moral control of the community. Each householder was supposed to discipline and instruct his family, but until schooling became general this duty could only partially be discharged. One of the questions to which we have no answer is whether householders in the seventeenth century did have regular family meetings for prayer and reading We know that these took place among landowners (who kept diaries) but not only are these occasional glimpses, they are glimpses of the more privileged and organized section of the population. But in the surviving minutes of kirk sessions, and these survive for hundreds of parishes, we can see the effective government of these communities, each holding the population of its parish in a tight structure of law and morality.

We have, of course, with this evidence, to allow for the error

1 Highland chieftains of the early fifteenth century: Duncan Campbell of Loch Awe in the centre, flanked by his sons. Portraiture was not yet a highly developed art in Scotland

2   Stirling in the late seventeenth century when towns were small, roads poor and the countryside near at hand for townsmen

3   The crowds watch the remaining elements of Scottish ceremony in 1883: the procession in Edinburgh of the Queen's Commissioner at the opening of the General Assembly of the Church

4　Armorial assertion and ceremony at an old-fashioned funeral: the procession for the burial of the 1st Marquess of Huntly in 1636

5　The political disturbances of the mid-seventeenth century in Scotland and England started with riots in 1637 in Scottish towns at the introduction of a new prayer book. The forms of worship played a large part in people's lives. Out of distaste for ceremony in church, men kept their hats on. 'Cricketts' were low wooden seats

The Arch-Prelate of St Andrewes in Scotland reading the new Service-booke in his pontificalibus assaulted by men & women, with Crickets stooles Stickes and Stones.

6 A Highland chieftain of the late seventeenth century in his best
clothes: probably John Campbell of Glenorchy, first Earl of Breadalbane,
as a young man. Fighting was still a necessary part of the life of a chief.
The 'kilt' at this date was merely a belted part of the great plaid

7 St Andrews University seal: St Andrews boasts the oldest of the Scottish universities and the seal asserts the association of the town with the patron saint of Scotland – a reminder that education was conceived as part of the structure of religion – and shows a class in progress

8 Execution in Edinburgh after the famous Burke and Hair trial in 1828 for obtaining corpses for dissection by murder. The trial provided a vivid picture of the criminal underworld of Scottish cities

9 A late English impression of Scottish ecclesiastical discipline in the days of church dominance. The English belief that all Scots wore tartan and lived in comfortable two-storey houses was equally far-fetched. The sabbatarian observance demanded by the Scottish kirk, though severe, never reached these heights and was enforced by non-violent punishments

10 A seventeenth-century representation of the nefarious activities attributed to an imaginary coven of witches in 1591. The most serious offence alleged was raising a storm which might have sunk the king's ship

11 A late, imaginary reconstruction of a witches' coven, equipped with the paraphernalia associated with witches: corpses, broom sticks, indecent undress. The devil as a bagpiper is a special Scottish touch

produced by sheer survival. Just as our impression of the quality of mediaeval building is distorted by the fact that those buildings we can see still surviving are those made well enough to survive half a millennium, so we know about kirk sessions only where they were active. Yet this includes a great many. One parish, St Andrews, had established its kirk session even before the Reformation was achieved, but for the most part the surviving documents date from periods after the establishment of a protestant ministry. The quality of a session depended considerably on the quality of the minister as a man of business. Not all ministers kept the parish book up to date, and not all the books, even when coherently filled in, have survived. They were at risk from the damp of bad housing and from the frequency of fires in crowded hamlets with thatched roofs. There are references, in periods of religious change, to their removal by ministers forced out from their cures. Given all these hazards the large number of kirk session registers that still survive from the 1630s and 1640s, or even earlier, show how systematic was this new instrument of social control. In East Lothian, for instance, out of 24 parishes records that predate 1650 survive from ten.[2]

The protestant revolution inserted two important elements into the nation's social structure. On the one hand it gave the country a professional class of clergy. A clerical class had, of course, existed under the old church, but it had not had the strong professional ethos or the united policy of this new one. Supposedly celibate, it had not been able to reinforce intellectual agreement with family ties. Now educated together in the same universities, in a narrow doctrinal curriculum, meeting together in the self-governing courts of the church at frequent intervals, sustained by the conviction of the performance of the inevitably successful purpose of God, the ministers formed an estate of the realm with a strong corporate spirit. Expounding the Word of God for several hours each week, visiting and examining their flocks, they had great powers over the mass of the people. As a middling class in society with an assured income they formed links by marriage or descent with the rising class of lairds.

The other feature was the holding down of society in the clamp of church discipline. From the pre-Reformation condition of a peasantry at the mercy of the nobility's arbitrary actions but relatively free of formal and legal restraints, Scotland passed to one where men were held as in a vice. The kirk session was a court, and not only did it have its own penalties of fines, penance, and in extreme cases, banishment, but it was backed by secular authorities, by town councils in the burghs and in many rural parishes by the baron court of the laird. A man could not escape the discipline of the kirk by moving. The parish in which he wished to settle would demand a testimonial of his conduct from the one he left. At odds with kirk and laird, his only way out would be to slip into a way of life regarded as lying outside decent organized society: become a soldier, a vagabond, go to sea.

The discipline the church enforced aimed at restraining the obvious sins of the flesh; drunkenness and brawling, fornication and other sexual irregularities came under censure. At first the idea appears to have been that a lapse into misbehaviour was an offence against the community, which required formal apology as well as other penalties before the offender could be accepted back into membership. In the case of fornication the sanction was refusal to baptize the child of the illicit union. The penal aspect of this discipline was stiffened and formalized. In 1589 St Andrews kirk session reduced the fine for fornication to 20s. in one instance, 'quhilk is ane half yeiris fie, being a puir boy'.[3] By then the puir boy and his girl would have had to appear for three Sundays running in sackcloth on the stool of penitence during sermon. The burden of shame for such offences may have intensified as the system became fixed, but it had become usual to keep the fine at 40s., so through the price rise of the last 30 years of the sixteenth century the financial cost of sinning fell, in real terms. In the seventeenth century it was the penance rather than the fine that hurt. It did not reduce fornication but it explains the number of cases of infanticide and abandonment of children.

Another major sphere of session control was 'the Sabbath'. In the early years of the Reformation the concern of the church about Sunday activities had been to put down those that were direct rivals with church attendance. But in the 1590s this changed to an insistence on the law of the Jewish Sabbath for the Christian Sunday. No labour of any sort should be allowed from Saturday evening. Sunday markets should be moved to other days. Later on it was recognized that Monday markets involved Sunday work, and they too were banned. Session records teem with penalties placed on people who worked on Sunday, who cut or ground corn, took their flax from the stream, carried peats, cut kail, cooked, or otherwise offended by using this day for work felt to be necessary. Sports and pastimes also were forbidden. It is not quite clear under which heading should fall the reproof — in the session book of Kingarth in the seventeenth century — of a man for beating his wife on a Sunday, but the reproof is there.[4]

How effective was this discipline? In certain matters of outward behaviour, remarkably so. The new concept of Sunday, not as a holiday with an obligation to attend mass, but as a day of devotion to serious behaviour, a turning of total energies from work to religion, was successfully fastened on Scotland, and the mark is still there. It implied at least intellectual assent to the doctrine of work, the idea that human life was a serious application to tasks for six days a week. The Calvinist church came in time to repress all other forms of break. There was no Scripture-based authority for commemorating Christmas, or other dates in the Christian year — even Pentecost — therefore such commemoration should be forbidden. Where in the past man had lived through a varied pattern of fast and feast in commemoration of events in the early church, the shifting of saints' days produced by the calendar against the weekly rhythm of rest and work resulted in an effect like that of the planets moving among the constellations; now he was held in a fixed and inevitable cycle of seven days. To break the notion of Sunday as a day of recreation the kirk at intervals put out orders for one or another Sunday to become a day of humiliation and fasting, which would be rigorously observed. Church discipline gradually won, but it could not totally repress the expression of remembrance of other feasts. 'Yule' continued to be the occasion of celebration, reproof and explicit prohibition until gradually Scottish allegiance was turned to the purely secular orgy of Hogmanay. And other dates — All Saints', Shrove Tuesday (fasten's even) — were even more regularly the occasion for orgiastic outbursts.

In other items of discipline success seems more limited. We have no statistical evidence for seventeenth - or eighteenth - century levels of unmarried pregnancy but it is clear from kirk session registers that there was a steady stream of such cases. There is no reason to associate with Scotland the remarkably low level found in the detailed study of Crulai in Normandy, where illegitimacy and pre-marital conceptions in the seventeenth century were less than 1% of births. We would, however, be going beyond the evidence if we were to assume that rural Scotland in the seventeenth century had the remarkably high level of unmarried pregnancy shown in some areas when civil registration of births started in the mid-nineteenth century.[5] What is clear is that the sanctions applied by the church did not succeed in making the population chaste. The attempt also to repress drunkenness seems to have been of limited success, to judge by the reiteration of denunciations, the accidents reported in some eighteenth-century parish registers, and the criticisms of visitors. These relative failures should not surprise us. Sexual and drinking customs are built into the pattern of communal life of a society and are not easily changed.

Kirk discipline had to allow a certain latitude to those of higher status. Only after the revolution of the seventeenth century could it be imposed on landowners, and it was never effective on the nobility. We find a member of the merchant guild of St Andrews let off sitting on the stool of penance for making his servant work on Sunday, but the servant made to serve his penalty.[6] The provost of Elgin in 1585 confessed to fornication but pointed out that 'repentance consistit not in the external gestour of the bodie or publict place appoyntit for samyn but in the hart': it was agreed that instead of public penance he should reglaze the north window of the church.[7] His plea shows that there was already established the peculiar cant of the reformed church. In 1680 the elders of Yester 'heard the sorrowful report (to the great griffe of the whole parochiners) of the fall of that hopeful young man Mr John Hay our Minister who had Committed fornication with Margaret Lamb his maid servant'. There was no question of public penance, but there was also no question of Mr Hay remaining minister.[8]

The new system of church discipline raises the problem of the efficacy of such rigid moral frameworks. The kirk evaded the danger of slipping into antinomianism by the creation of 'covenant theology'. That is, it transferred the government's method of persuading people to keep the peace by getting them to take on a 'general band' to do so, backing up generalized obligation with specific promises, to religious matters. Beginning in the 1590s, with increasing frequency, congregations would be asked to bind themselves in an agreement with God. After that, for all that Calvinism discounted totally the merit of works, they could be reproved for falling away from an explicit bargain.

This was an added resource in the battle against sin. A kirk session was not merely concerned with sin, it was concerned with all corporate aspects of life, with mutual support in time of need, and with behaviour which, if not directly sinful, could give rise to scandal. We find the early session records of St Andrews concerned to prevent women living alone, a state which created an assumption of immorality.[9] Some sessions would reprove parishioners for general uncharitableness or for being unneighbourly.[10] But generally the weakness of the kirk sessions' concern for morality sprang from the fact that they were courts, not confessionals. A session could discern and investigate the outward manifestation of sin, or at least of some sins, but not the sin itself. This was a particularly dangerous moral gap in a Calvinist society enthused with the concept of membership of God's elect. It became easy to ignore the fact that those who watched the penance of an offender in church on Sunday might be in greater moral danger than the penitent. It became possible for those conscious of God's assurance to feel that they were living as God wished, and from that it was a short step to spiritual pride. It became easy to equate morality with outward observance, particularly the confining of sexual experience to matrimony, and to believe that sexual offences were of a different order of sinfulness from other moral failures.

The kirk attempted to deal with offences, not with offenders. This meant that discipline should lie equally on the shoulders of all, not for any reasons of democratic theorising but simply because a lapse from moral standards was equally in all evidence of a life not lived by the guidance of the Holy Spirit. When strong enough it would try to impose its sanctions on the great, and it never accepted the idea that a different standard of probity was required of the two sexes. In this way, in the long run, in the very long run, it did something to encourage the concept of equality between the sexes. But in the short run its emphasis was very different. It enhanced the position of the father of a family, the head of the household. It is often thought that this was a result of the renewed emphasis of Calvin on the authority of the Old Testament. But Judaism has always had a considerable element of matriarchy. In the Old Testament it is women, not men, to whom divine authority is given to break the established sexual norms.[11] It would seem more likely that the patriarchal features of Scottish Calvinism came from the intrusion during the sixteenth-century changes of the accepted social priorities of Celtic society into religion. Protestant theology broke away from the Mariolatry which Italian practice had given to the Catholic church and there are signs that the adherents of male superiority in Scotland wished to go further. It is well known that John Knox could not envisage a situation in which women had authority with God's approval. 'God hath reveled . . . that it is more than an monster in nature that a woman shall reigne and have empire above Men.'[12] A little regarded sentence of the 1560 Confession of Faith shows that he was not alone among the reformers: 'We flee the society with the Papistical Kirk in participation of their Sacraments; first because their ministers are no ministers of Christ Jesus; yea (which is more horrible) they suffer women, whom the Holy Ghost will not suffer to teach in the congregation, to Baptise.'[13] The priorities in that sentence are instructive. The reformers took the easy line of thought in assuming that the foundations of their social system had divine approval, and that therefore it was the model to be followed by others. Celtic emphasis on masculinity thus acquired divine sanction. Hence came the tremendous masculine emphasis of Scottish social and ecclesiastical institutions in the seventeenth century, shown most revealingly in the way in which some parish registers record events of birth and death. The form 'James Allan, a daughter' and 'James Allan, his wife's death' are common, and the headship of the family might even be carried beyond the grave with 'James Allan, his relict's death'.

As we see Scotland change from a society relatively lacking in law and organisation, in which the bonds on most men took the form of simple disorganized oppression, to one of systematic, structured repression, our interest must naturally lie in assessing how far this tremendous change was carried out with the active support of the people concerned. This remains a question unanswered and unanswerable, but there is one significant pointer. Protestant Scotland in the seventeenth century produced practically no religious literature. It spewed out writings on the question of church government, some diaries in which religious experience is recounted in detail, the best known of these being that of Johnston of Wariston, and sermons enlarging on the relationship of men's hearts to God. None of this can be considered to have any literary value. There is not a word of it that could warm or illuminate the reader. In a century in which France produced the writings of Bossuet and Pascal, and England those of Donne, Bunyan and Herbert, lowland Scotland had nothing to offer. It was, of course, a small country with a small population. Men of genius do not occur often. But there are two bodies of poetry from seventeenth-century Scotland which merit serious attention, the *Carmina Gadelica* and the Border Ballads. The former is Gaelic poetry, which even when not expressly religious in theme is steeped in the symbols of religion. The latter is secular narrative: the other-world element in it is from magic, not religion. Both collections, as the accumulation of oral tradition, have elements from a wide range of time.[14] Their existence raises the suggestion that in the Highlands, where the new church had as yet practically no hold, men lived a life in constant association with religious imagery, and that in a part of the Lowlands where the new church had triumphed the imagination of men was held in a purely secular world. People assented to the kirk's outward discipline, but their imaginations were not kindled within its values. When the kirk destroyed the old pattern of commemoration, festival and fast that made the Christian year, and threw away the elaboration of ritual, it may have closed one channel for the imagination without opening a new one.

* * *

Besides religious and political revolutions the sixteenth century saw, all over Europe, the phenomenon of the price revolution. The impact of this in Scotland appears both less marked than elsewhere and contained within a shorter length of time, but it still involved difficult adjustments. The boll of oatmeal, the big grain measure which held about 140 pounds, varied in price in the first half of the sixteenth century round 9s. Scots; in the 1560s and 70s it varied drastically round about 14s., and in the 1590s over 65s.[15] Much of this change was simple currency depreciation of the 1570s and 1580s, but even when grain is measured against the genuine silver content of the coins, the price of the basic cereals had doubled between 1550 and 1600.[16] The most likely explanation of this change is population pressure, which receives support from the evidence of a fall in wages in real terms. Of course, in Scotland's primitive economy there were very few people totally dependent on money wages: it was more prestigious, as well as safer, to receive payment in kind. This makes it difficult to find a reliable picture of the movement of wages. Where we do get payments recorded for work done, as in burgh accounts, we do not know the scale of the work or the number of days it took. But in the accounts of the Master of Works for building and repairing the royal palaces[17] we have a collection of payments to a work force which is measured in numbers of men and numbers of days or weeks, and appears comprehensive. These show that in the 1530s the skilled craftsman (wright or mason) earned 15s. a week and the unskilled 'barrowman' 5s. In mid-century these figures were 18s. and 9s: at the end 60s. and 30s. In a period when the price of basic food had gone up seven times the wage of the skilled man had multiplied by four and of the unskilled by six. We do not know how far these price changes may have been compensated by other adjustments. There may have been relative falls in the cost of household necessities, clothing, salt or fuel, but until these are found we must accept the idea of the late sixteenth century as a period of pressure on the standard of living of those who worked for money, and of pressure particularly hard on the skilled worker. This is another pointer to the likelihood of population growth. The bargaining power of labour, particularly skilled labour, was low, and the assumption must be that this was because labour and some sorts of skill were abundant.

There are other indications of population pressure. One is the extreme bitterness of highland clan conflicts over land — though equally this may have been the result of the disorder produced in the Highlands by the systematic destruction by the crown of the dominant MacDonald power. Another pointer is the pressure on kindly tenants, and the decline in their status. The great emigration from Scotland between 1620 and 1640 also suggests the presence of surplus population.

If population was growing in the later sixteenth century, it was doing so under frequent difficulties of food supply. We have notes of food shortages for 1563, 1567, 1570, 1571, 1574, 1586, 1595, 1598 and 1600. These are all mentioned in the first volume of Chambers' *Domestic Annals of Scotland*. Research might show more, but it might also reveal that most of these were of local implication only. The troubles of 1570 were a dislocation of supply, not a real dearth: the mills could not grind because of frost. Probably the shortages of the 1590s were of general impact, for similar ones are to be found across Europe. We know too little about the birth-rate then to hazard guesses about possible changes in its level, but in undeveloped societies death is more variable in its incidence than births, and therefore more easily changed. So it is to a reduced impact of death that we would expect to assign any population growth that may have happened. This could have been produced by a better food supply, better in quality or, more probably, in reliability. Behind this would most likely lie better weather for growing crops. But there might also be the influence of more efficient farming. Certainly before the 1620s some of the peasantry in East Lothian and the Borders had learnt to lime their land. Even allowing for this, the most likely factor in population growth remains modification in the impact of disease. Infections may have come less often, or less fiercely. The general European story of epidemics suggests that if there was such an amelioration in the impact of infection, it ended abruptly in the mid 1590s.

Population may have been expanding up to the 1590s, but it seems very uncertain that it then continued. The rise in prices, which suggests such growth, had ceased by the opening years of the seventeenth century. We have glimpses only of an appalling famine in various parts of southern Scotland in 1623.[18] We do not know how many died, merely that in those places from which figures can be obtained, many did. The number of people in Scotland may have declined in the first half of the seventeenth century. Certainly many left in the 1630s. Men went abroad to fight in the German wars, to serve in the Swedish army, to eastern Europe too; and, in particular, the Scots took advantage of land-grabbing in Ulster in a big way. The king's commissioner there, Lord Strafford, guessed that there were as many as 50,000 Scots in Ulster by 1640. And in the 1640s Scotland experienced her last epidemic of plague, which struck the burghs and the neighbouring countryside and killed people in thousands. The pessimism of religious thought in the period after the Reformation should not surprise us when we remember the frequent experience of death and disaster.

Chapter 3

The Godly Community

'Hie upon Hielands and laigh upon Tay
Bonnie George Campbell rode out on a day
Saddled and bridled sae gallant tae see,
Hame came his gude horse but never came he.'

Bonnie George Campbell

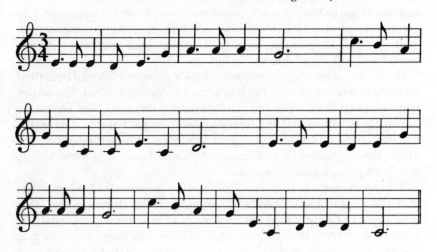

B Y the end of the reign of James VI (1625) the kirk had carried through the first part of the programme of the 1560 reformers in the Lowlands. Educated ministers expounded God's message in the parishes, imposing on themselves and their flocks a godly discipline by the machinery of the lower courts of the kirk, the kirk session at parish level and above it the presbytery. In doing so they carried out a policy implicit in the events of 1560, if not clearly laid down, the creation of a profession. The ministry made up a group with a common education, fulfilling a defined function and inspired by a clearly expressed body of belief in a language which already verged on jargon in its hackneyed use of biblical imagery. Ministers were often related by intermarriage, and reared their sons to the same profession. They were also linked with the lesser lairds by kinship as well as by belief. Like the lairds, and like most of society, they still took it as normal to be armed, but in fact already their personal safety relied less on force than on the accepted idea that they were particularly God's elect and should not have force used on them. As yet there was no fixed dress for a minister, but his status was apparent. Through the stresses and strains of the Great Rebellion of the mid-seventeenth century and the uneasy settlement that was imposed on the country after it, it is striking how rarely was violence done to any minister, however intemperate his language. The deplorable phrase, still sometimes used to describe a minister, the 'man of God' (deplorable because it implies that other men do not belong to God), came into use in this period.

The lairds, allies of the ministers, made a group which had benefited by the price revolution of the late sixteenth century. Their feu duties had remained fixed while the value of money changed, and were now negligible as a burden. King James's peace, for all that it had its limits, had been of benefit to both groups. Ultimately, though they opposed it at the time, Charles I's settlement of church lands and teind was to give both groups greater economic security.

But the movement from the Reformation incorporated things other than the aims of 1560. The Melvillian party in the church in the 1580s and later had brought forward the idea of a church self-governing and separated off from the machinery of the state. The new claims were to involve a reshaping of the church's own orders, so that it should have no separate rank of bishops, but should associate a permanent 'eldership' with the ministry. It is not the function of this book to retell the political history of the great storm that engulfed the three kingdoms of Scotland, Ireland and England between 1638 and 1660. It is enough to remember that the ministry played a vital part all through it, influential and intemperate, and for a brief time, 1649-51, with allies within the gentry, imposed the government of a chaotic and extremist dictatorship, the 'Whiggamore' rule.

What kind of a society did this church party manage to create in its short time of power? It had, all through the period of strife, control of the only 'mass media' of the day, sermons. Sermons were long and frequent, for there was preaching twice on Sunday, measured by a generous hour glass, and often on a weekday as well. Many survive in print. These may not be entirely representative of the *genre*, but they are the specimens that people thought particularly edifying, and their content tells us something of the aims and visions of the society that heard them. That they tell us absolutely nothing about conditions of social life, of the relationship of man to man, or of man to his physical environment, is also an illustration of the priorities of the church. The ministry scorned to preach about morals and behaviour: such were mere 'works', which without assurance of salvation were valueless. Its duty was to expound the great truths of God's revelation.

Material facts could not be ignored so totally by the rest of society. These years were a time of war: successful war at first, but later on came real fear to many lowland communities from Montrose's highland army and its incursions, and later still the successful invasion of Cromwell. They were years of bitter rivalry between highland clans and of savage reprisals by the Whiggamore dictatorship. War led to economic dislocation and material destruction that the country could not afford. It also coincided with the last major outbreak of plague, that of 1646. The period of dictatorship by the saints was a time of stress and fear, in addition to the inevitable stresses of a revolutionary situation. But it was also a period when the kirk can be seen endeavouring to complete and enlarge the scheme of a godly society set out in *The First Book of Discipline*.

This scheme had been for a serious God-fearing community living a life that showed outwardly the inner strength of divine assurance, searching the Scriptures to understand God's will and caring for the weak as part of Christian duty. Expressed more crudely this meant a programme of religious observance, education and poor relief. A great deal of study has been put by historians into the second of these categories, though often in work that lacks historical judgement, a little on the first[1], in so far as such things can be studied, and almost nothing on the last.

We know something about the form of worship in church but relatively little about organized worship in the home. That the Bible was to be read in both church and home was part of the Reformation ideal. But it is unlikely that at, say, mid-century, or even by 1700, the bulk of families had a Bible in the house. G. D. Henderson has shown a surprising number of occasions in which even the parish church lacked a Bible.[2] These instances are on record because the recording agency, kirk session or presbytery, was taking steps to remedy them. There may have been others not remedied. But at least the church was a place where a book could be kept dry. It would have a slated roof, and glass in the windows to keep out the weather. Most houses in the seventeenth century were damp, with turf roofs draining through the walls. Few people had furniture that could protect paper, such as chests or cupboards. The frequency with which kirk sessions in the seventeenth century used surplus funds to present portions of the Bible to poor children is a strong pointer against the existence of family Bibles. Books do not usually appear in testamentary inventories that survive from this period or

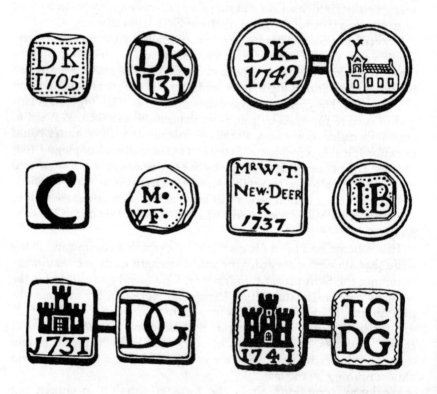

Scottish church tokens, used during the seventeenth and eighteenth centuries to regulate entry to the *annual* communion service. The tokens — struck from moulds and of lead or pewter and about the size of a coin — were locally produced, hence the wide variations in design (from the Proceedings of the Society of Antiquaries of Scotland 1940-41)

the early eighteenth century, but if there are any books in such a list the Bible is also sure to be mentioned. This shows that the Bible was the first of books, but still it was a personal possession, not in some special way a family one that would not be listed in the personal property of the dead. The emphasis on reading and expounding the Bible in church also implies that many people would not otherwise become acquainted with it. Not only were large portions read aloud, but it was used as a preaching text in a way which enforced detailed knowledge. Instead of the comparison of whole chapters or whole books, urged by Knox, the sermon technique was to take, for months on end, an 'ordinary', a single book. Sunday by Sunday, text by text, the minister would inch his way through this, expounding the various interpretations and elaborating the possible spiritual implications.

How complete was church attendance? This is a question that historians have tended not to ask. Discipline was effective at suppressing alternative recreations, though this required constant vigilance, and kirk sessions records contain frequent attacks on people for tippling in alehouses during sermon, allowing beggars to get on the road instead of going to church, and the like. Most parishes assigned to elders by turn the task of seeing that all who could be were at kirk, which implies a likelihood of some backsliding. On one occasion church records supply us with a more detailed picture of those at church, and it may be that others will be found to enlarge or correct the picture. In January 1640 the men in the parish of Dundonald reaffirmed the Covenant,[3] and this reaffirmation, about which there was nothing voluntary, was signed by those who could write their names, 42 in all, while marks were made for a further 180. Yet if we list the names of the men with whom the session records dealings during the year just past, the poor, the offenders against discipline, the witnesses in such cases and tradesmen carrying out work for the session, we can collect 40 names. Of these only 21 reaffirmed the Covenant. Some of the poor may have been sick or dead: moral offenders may not necessarily be the best of church attenders: it was a large parish and the time was deep winter. Yet even so the shortfall is surprising. We should be on our guard against the assumption that our ancestors were unanimously church attenders.

There is a problem of evidence also about the creation of the structure of parish schools. The country had already, by 1600, enough universities to produce the ministers needed for the reformed church and to give a secondary education to the young of the nobility. St Andrews was the university most favoured by the nobility in the seventeenth century. Students were treated in a method similar to a nineteenth-century public school, living together and being trained in religious principles as well as in formal learning. The weakness of the educational pattern in the early seventeenth century was that such students could be recruited only from private tuition or the burgh schools. There was then no parish school system to bring forward recruits from the peasantry.

Two Acts of Parliament in the early seventeenth century, of 1616 and 1633, laid down that each parish was to have a school provided by landowners. The volumes of the *Acts of the Parliaments of Scotland* contain many regulations that were never put into practice, and since these two Acts did little to indicate how the money was to be raised or in what quantities, what were to be the qualifications of teachers and what the subjects taught, one would expect that these would be among the failures. An enquiry into parish revenues in 1627 shows several parishes in southern Scotland demanding a school: 'Not ane of the paroche can read nor wryt except the Minister' is a typical entry from Mordington in East Lothian.[4] We have tended to take this as a general picture of the situation then, but it is quite possible that the answers to the enquiry, which was primarily about teind and church revenue, may have been deliberately distorted by a group of ministers anxious to get parish revenues increased by making the worst of the situation. Certainly by 1650 a school appears to be the norm in the parishes of southern Scotland. Sometimes these can be found mentioned clearly in session registers. There was the one in Dundonald which we know about because the session laid down in detail the timetable of the school day. Often, though, the only reference, years after a school had been established, may be a notice in the accounts 'to the schole-master for learning puir scholars'.[5]

It looks as if it was the period 1633-50 that saw the main work in creating schools. This, of course, overlaps the period of dominance by the church party and shows that clergy and landowners were working together towards the godly community. The parish school laid a financial burden on landowners, who had to provide a house and a salary for the schoolmaster, and on the peasantry who would pay small fees for their children. None of the sums involved were large, but none the less the acceptance of the effort involved when a non-literate population takes on such a burden is not to be belittled. We get some impression of this from a brief order in the session book of Kingarth on the island of Bute, which called on 'any elder that can reid' to inspect the work of the school. The young were to receive a social and spiritual benefit denied to many of the elders of the parish. 'The most pairt of these that has children for the schole is illiterat and knowes not the good of learning.'[6]

It may not have appeared exactly in that light to the young. Schooling began often at the age of six, and the scattered settlements of Scottish parishes meant that the school was a long way off for many of the children. They would walk it daily, each carrying a peat for the schoolhouse fire. The school day was long, lasting over eight hours, and though the regulations of Dundonald show that playtime was accepted, there were no play elements in learning. The disciplinary attitudes of Scottish Calvinism carried into the world of learning, and it was generally accepted that physical punishment was the route to knowledge. The children would be kept at school until they could read and write and had a sound knowledge of doctrine. It is difficult for people brought up in a society which takes formal education for granted to assess the effect of such development. True, not all children went to school. In a big parish there would be no single place where a parish school could be put to be in reach of all. But we can see from the figures of those who, at different dates, signed the Covenant that the population of the seventeenth century was in some places as advanced as later generations. For instance at Stranraer in 1643 88 out of 183 could sign their names: in 1760 96 out of 229. In mid-eighteenth-century ecclesiastical records we sometimes get the signatures of heads of families to 'Calls' to one or another candidate for the ministry, and these also show considerable numbers preferring not to use their own signature. But this is not a true measure of the more significant side of literacy, ability to read and understand. Reading and writing are skills not necessarily acquired together, and the retention of these skills once acquired depends on the opportunities of practice. People who did not occupy a position where they might have to render accounts might easily lose the ability to write yet still be able to read.

The usual parish school would contain both the children of the peasantry and of the gentry. This gave the schoolmaster an incentive to go beyond the rudiments of English, so that he might share in further tuition of the richer children. Schoolmasters were supposed to be qualified for further teaching in mathematics and Latin, and this qualification was often fulfilled.[7] A peasant's son who showed aptitude had a chance to pick up enough Latin to pass to the university, and the parishes subscribed towards bursaries to make this financially possible. University opened the career of minister to the persistent and lucky. Those failing in either of these qualifications, 'stickit' ministers, would provide the next generation of schoolmasters. Education thus opened the door, or at least set it ajar, to social mobility, and though the schoolmaster lived little better than a peasant the minister could enjoy some comfort. The rewarding careers in terms of money or power were still confined to those of a landowning family, but some peasant children could, and did, better themselves.

In the long run, the very long run, the ability of all classes to absorb the written word might have remarkable secular effects. In the short run, schooling provided the parish with the more efficient means of self-government. A body of elders who could read and write, keep accounts and make entries in the session book, was a body much more efficacious in its ecclesiastical function. The achievement of such a body, and the establishment of the normal working day in the lives of the children, also changed society deeply in both religious and secular terms. Work had always been accepted by the theology of the reformed church as a necessity of life, but in the unimproved agriculture of the seventeenth century many people in the country did not work regularly through the weekdays of the year. The discipline of regular work, at least for part of a man's life, as well as literacy, were the contribution of education to Scotland.

* * *

Education was a tremendous achievement. Poor relief is, in the long run, a less happy story. This lies partly in the different nature of the problem. The cost of education is foreseeable from year to year; in agreeing to furnish schools landowners were not signing a blank cheque. Eventually in the 1690s statute laid down that the cost of the school was to be shared between landowners and tenants, and in practice this method of splitting the cost was already accepted. Education is also a provision benefiting almost everyone. Poor relief, in a society liable to severe emergencies, is unforeseeable as a burden, and when such a society progresses to greater physical security the benefit acquires a selectivity which separates the interests of the givers from those of the recipients of welfare.

The Scottish Parliament had passed, in the 1570s, an Act for poor relief on the English model, which left the duty to the justices, the administrative unit to be the parish. Nothing in fact seems to have been done because of the Act, but already parishes which had established kirk sessions were channelling alms to the poor through these. A session did not need to be empowered by Parliament to take part in a matter fundamental to its concept of community and morality; it would collect for the poor after sermon, and normally assigned to them all other revenue, for instance that from fines. As well as this there was still unorganized charity, both the spontaneous humanity of humble folk who would take beggars into their homes or give them food, and also the tradition of largess to beggars on rites of passage. In the 1590s Parliament acknowledged the existence of the session as the main administrator of relief, but the aid given was not given because of legislation. Community and Parliament both recognized the basic need; their assessment of the best mode of relief might sometimes differ and sometimes be the same.

Traditionally the policy of Parliament was to distinguish between the poor, that is those too old or infirm or too young to be able to support themselves, and vagabonds and beggars, people who, whether in physical terms able to support themselves or not, had settled down to a life of vagrancy. It assumed that the distinction was total: people who wanted help belonged to one group or the other. If 'poor', they were to be sustained: if vagabonds, they were to be penalized, set to honest work under the threat of drastic punishment, and of course, sustained in it.

As twentieth-century governments know, this is an over-simplified distinction. It ignores the fact that beggars may have become such through necessity. Unemployment, even if the word did not yet exist, was already a fact in the sixteenth century. If a man had failed as a peasant farmer there might well be no work for him as a farm labourer for others, and no openings in the primitive industry of the day. Worse still, that industry was subject to fluctuations, not only the business cycle of confidence or retrenchment but also from sharp variations in harvest yield. A poor crop would mean severe shortage for most people and starvation for some. All available cash would be devoted to food. With no purchasing power available, the industries of the day, cloth-making, brewing, iron-working and so on, would close down. Those who lived by them would join the vagrants on the road, looking for work and begging. To draw a line between poor and beggars was to ignore that many beggars did not wish to be idle. Local communities worked in practice on a different distinction, that between 'our poor' and 'beggars from elsewhere', which had more reality in both fact and feeling. Both groups would receive alms if funds were available, but it was felt that 'our poor' ought to have preferential treatment. In practice when all that was available was inadequate, the importunity and immediacy of beggars might mean that they, and not the old and infirm, got support. In the towns a real effort was made to control 'foreign beggars', not by the draconian penalties laid down by Acts of Parliament but simply by stopping them at the gates.

This partially organized pattern of local relief in the hands of sessions worked well enough where the minister and session were active and the scale of the problem moderate, and seems to have been well established by mid-seventeenth century. It could not cope with the effects of famine or pestilence. In fact it is doubtful if even a much more sophisticated structure could have dealt with the famines of the seventeenth century. In 1623 we get glimpses of a disaster beyond the competence of local or central administration. Two failed harvests brought starvation and disease on a scale we can scarcely credit today. The few scanty records we have show people dying in hundreds in small towns where the normal population cannot have been more than a thousand or two. Even though in every famine there would be a pattern of movement from country to town, particularly since many towns were ports to which there was a faint chance of grain ships coming, the scale of the problem was appalling. The Privy Council appealed in a miscellaneous way to all elements of local administration to apply the poor law, control beggars, raise money by rates, make lists of the poor of each parish, give out food to the destitute on the same day each week (to prevent double relief), but the crisis was too great and too advanced. There was no work for artisans and labourers, and beggars swarmed the roads. As the Privy Council remarked 'the preposterous pitie of the cuntrey folk' made it impossible to confine alms to the local poor. The generosity of those nearly destitute to those totally so was unsuppressable.[8]

In the period of church dominance we can see poor relief working more effectively under central direction. In 1649 an Act of Parliament again demanded that parishes raise rates for poor relief, and since this coincided with a period of high prices and food shortage there was urgency behind the enactment. It seems that many parishes obeyed for the time of emergency. Later there was devised, Act by Act, a scheme by which Scotland would solve both her economic and social problems. Beggars were to be put in long, compulsory apprenticeships to industrialists and sustained, while they learnt a skill, by parish rates.[9] No move was made to obey. The whole scheme remained totally imaginary. Since providing work for the poor has never proved a cheap way of dealing with unemployment, and slave labour is notoriously inefficient, failure was no loss. But the emergency pressure of 1649-50 did leave its mark on the system of relief. In the second half of the century we can see parishes normally maintaining their poor by voluntary contributions, building up reserves for emergencies and assessing themselves when these reserves ran out. They were aided by a relaxation in the pressure of natural forces. Plague did not strike again. Though the years of war led to plundering and devastation and though crops were poor and the market structure of the country fragmented, the appalling picture of 1623 was not repeated. Not all parishes were well organized and not all had funds enough to cope, but some sort of approximation to the ideal of *The Book of Discipline* was being achieved.

All this, however, depended on variable elements. The 'system' worked when there was a real sense of solidarity between different groups in the community, constant pressure from the minister and a situation that had not got out of hand. Before the end of the century we can see places where the minister could not get the co-operation of his richer parishioners. In Spott, East Lothian, in 1686 the elders abandoned assessment for the poor because 'the last time they met with great difficulty and contempt' and now 'they judged it not worth their pains and very little for the poors behoof'.[10]

In the last general famine of Scotland, that of the 1690s, some communities held together and weathered the storm, some were overwhelmed and some failed to act together. Deaths were fewer than they might have been without mutual aid, but it should not surprise us that our scraps of evidence point to Spott as the place with the highest recorded mortality.

*   *   *

In various ways, then, we should regard the mid-seventeenth century as the period of fruition of the seed of the Reformation. The godly community was not always godly, but at parish level there was a real community and its achievements were considerable. Community extended between parishes, and disasters would lead to mutual help. One of the commonest of these was fires. Jumbled groups of thatched houses easily caught fire, particularly in towns. Kelso was burnt down three times in the seventeenth century. Appeals for those thus made homeless, for the welfare of prisoners of war or for other good causes, would be sent round the parishes and the response might be large contributions. Deserving cases of destitution would beg from parish to parish with a letter of recommendation from presbytery or synod, and receive generous alms. But this sense of community had strict limitations. Sections of the nation, occupational or geographical, lay outwith it.

The group most obviously excluded was of those who could not keep the moral code, the law of either church or state. Nominally a sinner was restored to full membership of the church after penance, and even before that he would be treated as within the fold. We can, for instance, find sessions paying relief to the mothers of illegitimate babies while proceeding against them as discipline cases for fornication. A session might also support a person while in gaol for a criminal offence. But we can also find executions for infanticide of girls unable to face the combination of shame and hardship that an unfathered child involved, and abandoned children, 'foundlings', provided a real problem of support in many parishes. Baptismal records sometimes note that children are base-born, and not in small numbers. One such entry records the name of the child — 'Nihil' — a forecast for its future. We can see couples in trouble with their session for irregular sexual activities forced to run away. The penalty for adultery, in terms of the number of occasions sinners had to appear on the stool of penance in church, was far more severe than for fornication. Irregular sexual activity that was not heterosexual was criminal and led to the death penalty. The diarist John Nicoll in 1650 records in Edinburgh the burning on Castle hill of a man and his victim, a cow, for intercourse; at various times Nicoll described gloomily the increase of crime in spite of brutal physical punishments.[11] From later in the century comes the story of a murder case at Wardlaw, near Inverness, where the chief suspect was tortured to obtain a confession. In spite of the fact that he lost his feet under interrogation he continued to deny the crime until his accomplice was caught: they were both then tried and convicted.[12] This was, of course, in an area of private jurisdiction, where the rights of the accused were scanty, but the central government might not have been more merciful. The Privy Council had the right to use torture, and though the councillors became squeamish about it, it was still put into practice for those suspected of political plotting or for those, such as Highland reivers, who were definitely felt not to be of the community.

This was also the period of the witch craze, and witches were *par excellence* people who had put themselves outwith the community. Here it is necessary to draw distinctions. Witchcraft in Scotland is a subject badly in need of anthropological and historical research, but even a casual acquaintance with its records suggests that it contained two widely separate types of offence. There was old-established folk witchcraft, the use of spells to help cure the sick, make butter, control animals and so on, that had run as an undercurrent to Christianity for centuries, sometimes using scraps of Catholic ritual or phrasing. A lot of this, though not all, was beneficient in aim: some was even automatic and innocent of all intention. An episode at Penninghame (Newton Stewart) in Galloway as late as

Witches before James I (VI of Scotland)

1706 shows this last type. The session heard that one woman had burnt the bedstraw of a man after death. This, to her, automatic act of hygiene and tidiness brought down a thorough parish investigation.[13] The records of the presbytery of Dingwall show in Applecross and Lochcarron the continuation of a whole pagan sub-culture of local rites, an investigation which clearly roused a genuine anthropological interest in the presbytery's clerk.[14] The General Assembly had classified witchcraft as illegal in the 1570s, and this general prohibition applied to both folk witchcraft and actions of more malicious kinds, but it was put out with little emphasis for the witch scare had not then struck. Charming continued, partly because in some areas, such as the Highlands, the hold of the reformed church was slight, elsewhere because it met, or appeared to meet, real social needs. In 1671 for instance, the parishioners of Yester were discovered by the session to be in the habit of going up to town to consult a wizard in the Canongate about thefts. For a small fee he would direct their suspicions. When a case of this was denounced in church the habit spread, and in the end the session had to let off offenders with nothing more than a private censure.[15]

Besides this there was criminal witchcraft, the witchcraft of the crazy theology of the day, criminal trial and execution, the witchcraft associated with the search for power, malice and evil doing, and intercourse with the devil. This seems to have caught on with James VI's panic in 1590 over cases in North Berwick, though there had been occasional outbreaks before, and was a really nasty business, containing a vast mumbo-jumbo about sexual dealings with the devil, covens, sabbats and some deplorable notions of legal evidence. Altogether, over a century or so, it led to some 3,000 trials, much torture and a lot of executions. Many of the accused were old women, the poorest and most defenceless part of society, but no one was immune. If accusations began in any area they were apt to spread and sweep in a whole collection of unpopular people, and at some time or other probably every parish had its cases. When, later in the century, the courts became sceptical and slow to act, there might be lynchings.[16]

Much effort has recently gone into discussing the general European causes of this craze, which seems to have reached its height at different dates in different countries. This is an exercise of doubtful productivity. In any system of criminal accusation when standards of evidence are abandoned and torture and delation are used, cases will abound: the obvious parallel is the spread of the Great Purge in Russia in the 1930s. Calvinist theology had abandoned the idea that the physical universe is controlled by general principles laid down by God in favour of the idea of constant and active intervention by spiritual powers. Everything that happened was the direct result of superhuman force. In such a theology it became easy to find a place for the direct intervention of the devil as well as of God, and with such a concept admitted there were bound to be enough disasters and causes for fear to keep a system of investigation alive. After 1660 the details of belief in witches and warlocks seem to have been more readily swallowed by Covenanters than by the established church, though both sorts accepted the general idea that witches existed and were potent. It has recently been suggested that in England witchcraft accusations were made by someone who had failed to respond to a request for some sort of aid or charity and subsequently felt a guilty fear of reprisal. The replacement of spontaneous alms-giving by the institution of the poor law would be the source of an increase in such affronts since it marked a decline in neighbourliness.[17] This does not seem a valid explanation for trends in Scotland, for the years between 1630 and 1670, which seem to have been the main period of witch trials, were the years when the parishes created a viable poor law that blended private charitable giving with compulsory elements, and in which assessment never took over for long enough to supersede the general Christian obligation of neighbourliness.

Besides those alleged to have allied with the powers of darkness to harm their fellow men, people whom all good churchmen outlawed from the godly commonwealth, there were others excluded who, if criminals, were no more so than were those left within acceptable society. The striking example of an excluded group in the seventeenth century was the labour force of mines and saltworks. There were various attempts in sixteenth-and seventeenth-century Britain to impose some sort of industrial slavery on the vagabond population, an instance of which was the legislation already mentioned, but this was typical of such attempts in remaining a dead letter. By contrast, serfdom on coal workers grew up not from legislation but from judicial decisions and the assumptions of lawyers.

An Act of 1606 had laid down that such workers should not be allowed to leave one employer for another without the consent of the first. This in itself would not have justified the assumption of unfree status which grew from it and was extended also to wives and children of the workers. What enforced serfdom was the basic assumption that the owner of an expensive piece of capital development had superior claims on the law to those of his work force. He needed labour and his needs had priority. Serfdom sprang from this prejudice. For a time it was also extended to the workers in lead mines. The type of serfdom was not the old agricultural tie with the land, but much more personal, a tie of the miner as property to his employer, and so more than halfway to slavery, and resembled that in Russia. It cut the mining community off from the rest of society, and this separation continued long after the ending of serfdom in 1799. Other people would not enter the occupation or marry into it under this system where women and children could be listed as part of the property of a mine, or whole families sent to work for another mine-owner when their owner did not need their services. In some places miners might not be buried in the common churchyard. Serfdom could never have arisen without certain basic social facts. One was that long and arduous work of a regular pattern was still unfamiliar and unattractive. A labour shortage would not necessarily be ended by generous pay. And the needs of property were more important to the lawyers than the rights of the individual.

It is not only in the mines in seventeenth-century Scotland that we move away from the modern image of society of legal equality, of discipline and regular work and of the privilege of law and order. The Northern Isles were only gradually becoming culturally a part of Scotland. In 1614 James VI ended the dictatorship of Earl Patrick there and began the attempt to replace the rule of his cousin with his law. That Orkney was still Scandinavian in folk ways is shown by the departure of many of her people to Norway in the famine of 1635. It was till very recently the reaction of people in northern Scandinavia to move northwards and coastwards when crops failed. The sea is more fertile than the land in the high latitudes.[18] The population of Shetland was even further from assimilation. Both islands were under vestiges of Danish law and their court books give an impression of authoritative government. In 1602, for instance, the gentry of Shetland put forward claims in essence similar to those of the mine-owners. They needed labour, and therefore people were not to leave the islands to work elsewhere. The courts maintained elaborate structures of mutual guarantee as a minimal way of seeing that peace was kept, the same policy as that followed by the Privy Council in dealing with highland chiefs. Men might not set foot on the holm of another: the holms were unoccupied islands given over to sheep pasturage, and a visit to one would presume an unwholesome interest in someone else's sheep. Nor might they walk through the land of neighbouring townships with a dog.[19] It is clear that in the Northern Isles the whole framework of law-keeping was a brittle thing, and the law had to be stern.

A main element surviving from older society was everywhere the place and function of the great houses. It was shown in the state of Aberdeenshire in the 1630s. Here the great house was that of Gordon, but besides Gordons there were the lesser aristocrats and greater lairds living a life that paid very little attention to any idea of equal obedience to the law. The nobleman rode abroad still with many men at his back. His household was full of hangers-on who were not servants in any real domestic sense. He would arm them when he needed to, and he was expected to keep open house on a grand scale for his tenantry or other people at hand. His presence and influence might be important in persuading lesser folk to settle their quarrels. The great feud over the burning of the tower of Frendraught which raged across the shire from 1630 began on the occasion when Huntly, the head of the house of Gordon, sent one of his sons on a journey there with Crichton of Frendraught and Gordon of Rothiemay, to pacify these two, and Rothiemay and the young noble died at night in the fire. The central government was too uncertain and ineffective to end the bitterness between Huntly and the Crichtons. Feuding and rapine, the organized intrusion of highlanders on to Crichton lands went on for several years.

In the southern Lowlands the keeping of old-style state was already declining. Ben Jonson's friend John Taylor, who claimed to have come gallivanting round Scotland in 1618, spoke of the nobles keeping 30, 40, 50 servants or perhaps more, and of feasting their fellow noblemen and followers for days on end.[20] But the numbers involved in lowland affrays at this time show that these followers were already more for prestige than for protection. Even so, this old fashion of life was an affront to the standards of the godly community. Followers of this type were not there for work: standards of cleanliness and service, even in the great houses, were low. Their existence was also a reason for the continuing poverty of the kingdom. But in the Borders and the Highlands they were also a danger to peace. The pacification of the border clans, made possible first by the end of war with England and then by the Union of Crowns, did not go on very fast, and seems to have held up altogether in the 1630s. New Commissions for enforcing law were issued by Charles I, but border reiving began again during the disturbances of the 1640s until Cromwell put an end to it once and for all.

In the Highlands and the areas that fringed them old-style lordship and clanship were serious problems for government. Life there had its pleasurable aspects. Taylor was taken by the Earl of Mar on one of the great highland hunting parties in which several hundred men would organize an enormous drive of game, and at the end of each day's slaughter all would picnic together, with the spits turning, the pots bubbling and the wine and aqua vitae flowing. Even when not on a special party, standards of consumption were high for those with wealth. French wine could be had cheaply. Lord Lovat, who is described as keeping a great family at vast expense, had his claret delivered at his door at Beauly in exchange for his pickled salmon. The chief's son, Simon Fraser of Inverallochy, was using in 1619 seven bolls of oatmeal (a boll would weigh about 140 pounds), seven more of malt and one of wheaten

flour every week for his household, besides eating his way through
70 cows a year and other meats. Before the century was out these
quantities were to seem fantastic to the Highland chronicler. And
the men who hung round even a lesser chieftain were not there
simply for prestige.

The clan marked the dominant 'alternative society' in seventeenth-century Scotland. There are several different meanings
to the concept of clan. Both in the seventeenth century and the
twentieth century, myth as well as truth is embodied in the theory
of the institution. The base of clanship was kinship, but that had
been extended and elaborated upon. Many of those who thought
themselves kin of their chiefs were no such thing: yet the claim to
kinship had a reality in that all participants believed in the myth and
acted upon it. Besides those who claimed kinship and had a
common surname with the chief there were often septs within the
clan of a different surname, sometimes with special functions. Some
surname groups spread across more than one clan. The clan was a
society theoretically of one kinship group which could enfold other
similar structures. The chief was its father. But by the seventeenth
century his authority had become something more political. There
had in the past been a real place for discussion and for the opinions
of the heads of the cadet branches and other sections of the clan, the
leading lesser men, *daoine uaisle* which lowlanders transliterated
as 'dunniewassalls'. In the largest clans this still survived. Without
this more dispersed political authority these would have dis-
integrated as had the MacDonalds as a unit 150 years before. The
great chiefs had learnt something from the fall of the MacDonalds,
and avoided too open an autocracy. But there is little survival of this
in the smaller clans, except during a chief's minority. There the
loyalty a chief had come to expect was absolute, and the obedience
great, covering everything except actions obviously inimical to the
interests of the clan as a whole.

We should admit then that the clanship of the late sixteenth and
early seventeenth century was a very different matter from the tribal
leadership found all over Scotland in the middle ages. Chiefs had
become autocrats, and their control over the clan lands ownership,
tempered only by a social and economic conservatism which
prevented them from trying to exploit it. When and why this
transformation had taken place is obscure. I would hazard a guess
that the time was the early sixteenth century, a time of obvious
political and economic stress in highland society. It is possible that
formative influences were the model of feudal lordship, already
established in the Lowlands and intruded into the Highlands by the

Crown, and the military needs of a period of strife. The effect was to turn many of the lesser chiefs into irresponsible prima donnas, pursuing their own power and prestige with very little concern for the welfare of the men whose loyalty was their chief weapon.

The policy of the Crown had been to encourage further the transformation of clan chiefs into landowners and feudal lords, to place responsibility on them for the behaviour of the clan, cut them off from the more inconvenient elements of Celtic culture and enhance their links with lowland society. It was a simple form of cultural imperialism. In the early sixteenth century Major had written of the division of Scots into 'Wild Scots' and 'householding Scots'. In James VI's view it was a division between civilization and barbarism. The mainland highlanders were 'barbarous for the maine part' and the islanders 'alluterlie barbares, without any sort of civilitie'. [22]

The reason for this lowered estimate of highland civilization proceeded from the fact that between the dates of the two judgments lowland society had made considerable progress in the direction of law and order, while highland society had stepped towards renewed barbarism. The period had not just been one of war, but, by all accounts, one in which feuds had been carried on without respect for accepted moral codes. Slaughter of all ages and both sexes took place, churches were no longer sanctuaries but might be burnt down with congregations inside them, treachery was used even to guests and within the immediate family. Some of this ferocity was a result of the changing nature of clanship. Since clansmen offered unquestioning loyalty to their chief, a quarrel between two chiefs extended mercilessly to the whole clan of each. In so far as some of the quarrels were about lands and lordships, slaughter at least reduced the pressure for revenge.

The central government showed its hand in the statutes of Icolmkil of 1616, a treaty forced on chiefs in the south-west by a moderate display of the sort of treachery they freely used towards each other. The terms were enlarged in Acts of Parliament. Chiefs were to dismiss their bards and to send their sons to be educated in the Lowlands. They were rationed in the number of 'household gentlemen' they could keep around them, and in the hogsheads of wine they could consume, a blow at the open entertaining of the great household. They were encouraged to have fixed residences and to invest in these as country mansions. It was under such influences, for instance, that McLeod of McLeod started to plant an orchard and make his castle at Dunvegan comfortable. Some houses, more easily in touch with the Lowlands, had already moved in this direction. *The Black Book of Taymouth* shows that the Campbells of Glenorchy were already well supplied with hangings, furniture and silver.[23]

Given the government's cultural assumptions, crude but not unjustified, this seemed the easiest and most painless method of pacification. Even the chiefs lived in conditions so primitive that it was but a slight change for the worse if they went on campaign. When we find Lochiel in the 1650s losing his silver spoons when Glencairn raided his camp, we see that his mode of life changed very little between home and the field.[24] The practices of hunting, cattle-droving and cattle-stealing inured clansmen to the hardships of campaigns. All that they needed to make them into superb fighting instruments was practice in the actual handling of weapons, and many chiefs, their imaginations stirred by the poems of the bards about ancestral warfare, specialized and took pride in this. The fact that highland armies in the mid-seventeenth century used bows and arrows is a reminder not only of the monetary weakness of the highland economy which made it difficult to afford the cost of guns, powder and shot, but also of the fact that they contained skilled fighters. It takes much more practice to handle a bow than a musket.

The reverse side of government policy was that it would eventually mean, and did, the cutting off of the chiefs from the culture of their people. This was a process already on the way by 1700. By the mid-eighteenth century almost all chiefs lived double lives, as chieftains and as lowland landowners, according to which had advantages at any moment. Further pressure to drop the chieftain side became sharp after the 1745, and as a result many of the heads of highland society were unable or unwilling to guide their people through the transformation into a modern economy and society.

Not all the blame for this should lie with the central government, for much of it was inevitable. If we look at different parts of the Highlands in the seventeenth century we can see various stages in the acquisition by chiefs of the benefits and outlook of lowland aristocrats. The Gordons, though they held feudal superiority over large highland areas were already lowland aristocrats with merely an abnormal ability to arrange hunting parties and call on men for war. In Sutherland they had acquired the dukedom, and so were foreigners to their clansmen. The Campbells were more genuinely highland in their culture and ambitions, but the head of the clan, the Earl of Argyll, spent much time and energy in national politics under Charles I. Fostering, the placing of the son of the chief as an infant in the household of a leading vassal, was still practised by his house in the 1620s, but consciously, and more as a means of making sure that the future Great Marquis should speak Gaelic than as a means of securing the total allegiance of his foster father, Campbell of Glenorchy, to his interests. McLeods and Lovats still used fosterage in its traditional way, but the Frasers of Lovat were, in both the seventeenth and eighteenth centuries, conspicuously successful combiners of the advantages of the two cultures. We have a description of the funeral of Simon, Lord Lovat in 1633 which was attended by the chief of the McKintoshes and 600 clansmen, of Grant and 800, of 900 McKenzies, 1,000 Rosses, 1,000 Frasers and another 1,000 of assorted clans.[25] Even if the figures have suffered highland exaggeration, they at least show the ritual a Lovat felt entitled to: 'Splendid in ashes and pompous even in the grave'. We need not think that the individual clansmen of Grant or Ross came to pay personal respects: they came because their chieftains wanted to show their force. The Lovat lords kept not a household but a court, to which the sons and daughters of lesser gentlemen were sent for their social education. Yet both Frasers and McKenzies would visit the south as ordinary noblemen, and the latter were turning to the law for careers for their sons.

There were still chiefs who acted in the old-fashioned way as fathers to their clan. One such, described by Martin Martin, in his *Description of the Western Islands of Scotland*, written in the 1690s, was McNeill of Barra. He arranged marriages for the widows in the clan, restocked his tenants with cows and took into his own household those too old to work their farms. Yet even he had a second side to his life apart from his clan. It is typical that he was away when Martin visited Barra.

The great state of the chiefs, the military emphasis, the prevalence of cattle-stealing, the idleness that was inescapable for many of the Highlanders for large parts of the year, the claims to good birth of tatterdemalion cattle drovers or stealers, all were signs that this society was not the godly community of the Reformed Church. The church made little effort to bring its gospel to the Highlands, but was not totally inactive. The first book printed in Scottish Gaelic was the Bible. We can see from the Fraser chronicle how clanship prevented peaceful life. We have the scene of the riot in Inverness in the 1660s, which grew from the failure of the chiefs to discipline their own followers themselves and their refusal to allow others to do it for them. In 1646 the minister of Killerlan had to leave his cure because he was a Fraser and his flock were McKenzies, while the clans were at odds.[26] The church did not manage to infuse society with the new theology except where, as in Campbell territory, the chief actually promoted it. Even where Protestantism was accepted men still lived in the daily presence of magic. Martin shows that the telling of tall stories about second sight was a favourite occupation in all the Western Isles. The minister of Wardlaw in the late seventeenth century described the land as suffering under bad crops so long as the blood of a murdered man was unavenged.[27] The islanders of north Lewis sacrificed to a sea god at Hallowtide by pouring a cup of ale into the sea before their drinking orgy.[28] Local gods or goddesses had to be propitiated by special rites at special places, magic wells or magic trees.

That highland culture would eventually be forced to give way to lowland became clear in the middle of the seventeenth century when Cromwell subdued the Highlands by force and built his fortresses at Inverlochy (now Fort William) and Inverness. Since Scotland and England were now inextricably joined in their political affairs, the power of lowland society was reinforced from beyond the border. It was not entirely unwelcome. 'Truly they civilized and enriched us' says the minister of Wardlaw of the English soldiers at Inverness. This show of force was not maintained, and the Highlands were left to more occasional and haphazard methods of restraint and control after 1660, but it indicated which of the two societies in Scotland would eventually dominate.

— Chapter 4 —

The Ramifications
of Poverty

. . . the many hundred inhabitants . . . daily seen in our streets without shoes and stockings, in whose looks care and a sense of dependence are expressed, who are actually starving for want of employment.'

David Loch (1778)

I T is a commonplace of social observers today that poverty is a trap: once in, there are built-in obstacles to getting out. It is also well known that among the poor the lines dividing people from one another, the lines of the social scale, are firmly defined. Both these facts can be seen in the Scotland of 1700. Nations can be poor as well as individuals or families, and the trap is as sure. The basic problem of an undeveloped nation in a world of richer societies is that its economic life is rudimentary in structure, so that none of the separate areas of economic activity can develop until a more elaborate network binds the whole together. This was so for Scotland. But within her crude structure there were sharp differences in wealth and status, and clearly demarcated functions. People were not equal. It is only in a society possessed of wealth or a strong administration that equality can be established. In seventeenth-century Scotland equality was not considered a desirable end. Men were not equal in the sight of God, for between the elect and the reprobate stretched an unbridgeable chasm. They were not equal in the sight of the state. Landowners, 'heritors', had rights and privileges, as well as duties, assigned to them by law. Burgesses similarly had their own privileges, though these were crumbling. Anyone in a dependent position, a servant or a farm labourer, was inferior in status to the poorest tenant who worked for himself. We can see some of these and other distinctions in the arguments in the eighteenth century about who ought not to be counted as 'heads of households' to take part in the Call to a proposed minister:

a beggar on the Charity roll, he has no family.
...was banished for sheep stealing.
...a single woman seldom at home and several times serving others.
...no better than she should be.
...a beggar partly maintained by the session.
...her husband fugitat for Murder.[1]

These are the prejudices of a propertied world. But even at kirk session level morality had to give way to the claims of property. A farmer was regarded as entitled to house a woman farm servant even when there was evidence of sexual misconduct with her because he could not manage without her labour.[2] Since existing inequalities in wealth were regarded as necessary and desirable, aid to poor people was not intended to put them on an economic level with others. As the risk of disaster in which all might share became less, so poor relief became less a form of mutual aid and more a dole from those who have to those who have not.

The seventeenth-century achievement of relative law and order meant that distinctions in degree became clearer. The aristocracy saw less fulfilment of its ambitions in the role of local magnates and more in that of British politicians. They began in the reign of Anne to see London as exclusively the source of power, office and wealth, even if the sphere in which they hoped to exercise power was still Scotland. Governments were made in London and their creation paid much more attention to English than to Scottish politics. Even the great house of Argyll, which continued longest to draw from its base of local strength, produced in the 2nd Duke (1703-43) a man whose wife was English and whose ambition was to be Commander-in-Chief of the British army. The London fixation of the ambition of the great nobles became clear after the Act of Union in 1707, and left the area of local power in Scotland to the gentry.

The class of gentry or lairds had first shown themselves of political weight in the struggles of the mid-seventeenth century. After 1660 they found a new social role. They provided the new group of lay professional lawyers. Advocates in the seventeenth and eighteenth century were almost entirely drawn from them, and from the advocates came the judges. This professional group was never as clearly defined an order as the clergy, but even if it could not claim a divinely based function it had much to mark it out from others. It enjoyed the organization of its own 'Faculty', the increased elaboration and development of the law it served, a common education, often in a Dutch university, and a way of life alternating between the courts and clubs of Edinburgh during law term and its private estates in vacation. It was a satisfying existence for a man of articulate intelligence. The lairds were also involved in trade. The backward economy which led to so many rents being paid in kind forced this on them, and the fact that the most buoyant sections of trade and industry (cattle, linen and coal) were all rural-based gave them a further impulse to this. The presence of a few seats in the Westminster parliament for lairds gave an edge to ambition. If a Scottish gentleman was to achieve a pattern of spending suitable to the scale of his landowning and political influence in English terms, he had to enlarge his revenue by trade or by the exploitation of mineral wealth or by an official salary.

The relations of a laird to his tenantry changed less readily than those with society above him. Estates often lay in baronies, and in these the baron court gave him a mechanism for the control of the minutiae of local life. He would have the opportunity of church eldership too, unless debarred by dissent, and in any case as a heritor he had a considerable say in the church's finances. Below him were his tenants. The richest of these were the occasional farmers of unusually large farms and the tenants of the single piece of expensive equipment on every barony, the local mill. Most farms were divided between several husbandmen at this time, but cases where a single family was directly responsible for a unit of land on its own were becoming much more common. We can study one in an inventory from Longniddry, East Lothian, of 1709. The farm appears to have had over 140 acres of arable, worked by 18 horses and 8 oxen, and with another ten beasts and eight carts. It even had a recently planted orchard; the farmhouse had at least five rooms and there were several outhouses. The inventory lists 11 beds, and since beds were usually shared, we must assume a good labour force living with the farmer. We can see touches of gracious living, a looking glass, an oak cupboard, a folding table and a considerable *batterie de cuisine*. There was the full apparatus for roasting on a spit, a frying pan, a brander or grill and a girdle for baking, as well as kettles, pots and pans. There was also a mustard box and a range of different sizes of stoup or tankard. The impression of a big household is supported by '21 peuther plates, 2 ashets, 4 Duzon of Trinchers' and another dozen of timber trenchers, as well as by a big table with forms on either side of it and two chairs. Master and mistress would sit at each end in the chairs and eat their meals with their farm servants off pewter or wood, drinking their own ale. In another part of the house, 'the North Roume', which seems from the quality of the feather beds and curtains, and from the housing of its chamber pot in a box, to have been the master bedroom, were kept the special treasures: 18 horn spoons and 3 silver quaichs, and chests full of linen, of sheets, pillowcases, tablecloths and napkins. The family even had some drinking glasses, and also 'ane house bible' and some other books worth 6 pounds Scots altogether. Life was still cramped enough for there to be beds in every room including the kitchen. Most of the long list of possessions pertained to the household as a unit of production: equipment for farming, for malting and brewing, for dairying, for spinning and weaving, for storing food as well as creating it: bee skips, pigs and geese all added to wealth. The instruments of self defence, 'two old guns and 2 pistols' also show a necessary concern of the farmer.[3]

From almost the same date we can find an inventory from the other side of the country showing a different unit of production and a very different way of life. This is that of William McGuffog, made in 1705. He lived, apparently with his farm servants, two men and a woman, in a single, squalid room in Galloway. He farmed some 45 acres of arable and owned 30 beasts beside his plough team, so he had capital. But that, and the minimal equipment necessary for processing and preserving production, was all his wealth. The household possessed one candlestick, one feather bed, three pairs of sheets and a single chamber pot. The servants presumably slept on straw, and nobody could have a change of sheets. Meals could be made by grilling or boiling, and were eaten off three pewter plates and nine timber trenchers, but at least the single 'little table' would be furnished with a cloth. The household made beer and butter and salted beef in a barrel, but these may well have been tainted by the presence in the same room of leather being dressed. Yet even McGuffog had his touch of luxury. The list gives him six shirts and six cravats, even if only one pair of shoes and two pairs of stockings, and he had a smoothing iron to keep shirts and cravats neat. He too was armed with a sword and a pair of whingers. No bible or books appear in the list.[4]

Of the two insights into ways of life, it is the East Lothian farmer who is exceptional. Below both men would extend a large body of lesser folk, some direct tenants of the laird, some sub-tenants of farmers, labelled by various names of which cottar seems the most generally used. A cottar might farm some land but he would have to draw most of his support from working on the land of others, whether as a labourer to the miller or a farm servant. His status and security would be the greater the more that his payment came in kind and the less in money.

The preference for income in grain rather than in cash was prudent in a period of undeveloped marketing and sharply fluctuating prices. It also reflected the ethos of personalized service rather than the more complex type of society where relationships are defined in elaborate gradations of tasks and rewards. Service as well as rents bound tenants to their landowners. There were complicated obligations in all rentals: provision of harvest workers, the carrying of peats and other goods, the duty to help bring in new millstones, all sorts of interruptions which controlled the farmer's use of his own or his family's time. A baron court could also enforce restrictions which might be inconvenient: the obligation to use the barony mill, the prohibition on selling products such as hay and straw outside the barony. The distinction between a tenant and a servant was not entirely clear-cut, for a servant might get his pay partly in the use of pasture and his duties were often of generalized service rather than specific tasks. There is a description of Sir Ewen Cameron of Locheil staying at Dunstaffnage in 1675 with the Earl of Argyll. Because he had not shaved for several days the Earl's valet shaved him in the presence of the Earl — an interesting comment on country house grooming and drawing-room behaviour — though Locheil had a servant with him whose task this was. Two of Locheil's clansmen stood by, as general hangers-on, watching uneasily.[5] In the 1680s Sir John Clerk of Penicuik in Midlothian, a substantial country gentleman of mercantile background, made a note of the servants he kept. The list of men reads '1 hynd, 1 man to help, 1 to thresh in the winter, 1 to look to the work horse and goe at sleds, 1 garner, 1 groom, 1 man steward, 1 man to wait on myself, in all 8 men at 30 Lib per head yearly'. These have fairly unspecific tasks, but they are a good deal more precise than those of the women: '1 nurse, 1 chamber maid, 1 cooke, 1 woman to wait on the children, 1 darie woman, 1 old wyfe to look to the hens and tell old tails to the bairns, 1 to wait on my wyfe, in all 7 at 20 Lib. per peice.'[6] It is surprising to see so small a force devoted to the task of house-cleaning in a substantial country household. The main function of a servant was to wait on a particular individual, or on a collective such as the hens and the bairns, not a set task about the house in a well-ordered and complicated structure. This partly explains the quantity of dirt so freely commented on by English observers in Scotland. It was nobody's special duty to clean any particular part of the house.

Such a servant system was, of course, only possible in the old type of upper-class housing: the tower house or other half-fortified building where rooms were few, interconnected and of multi-use, and much of personal contact went on in some central hall open to all. But by 1700 a new type of country house was being created, the elegant palladian or classical quadrilateral of measured proportion with, in some sophisticated versions, outflung wings. The change was not merely a step in visual sophistication and delight: it was a new concept in gracious living. Such a house would separate off menial activities, preferably into the wings, and even in the central block there would be a separation of functions and ways of life between state rooms and others. The new invention, the corridor, gave separate access to the different rooms. The hall ceased to be the centre of life in the house and became merely an entry place. Privacy, separateness, cleanliness and display all became possible on a new level. Servants would occupy servant quarters, and care for the house as well as for its occupants. Country houses of this kind would be centres of economic stimulus, requiring goods and the services of craftsmen. Even if they were as yet only occasional in the landscape it was a significant change.

Town life, at least in Edinburgh, was also creating a more complex pattern of life, and emphasizing the relationship of cash rather than of service. In the Privy Council records of 1701 we can find a scheme, put to the Council for approval, which illustrates the new pattern of service, and also shows why towns regularly had the reputation of encouraging vice. 'It is well known that the leidges have been much imposed upon by having dishonest and profligat servants recommended to them by wedmen, wedwifes and others not qualified . . .' says the application for approval; 'advertisements in gazetts . . . are in no ways sufficient' as a means of getting information. Unlicensed intermediaries should be forbidden, and servants should have to produce 'testificates of their fidelity and Christian deportment'. Wet nurses too should show if they were married, and if not, at least certificate 'that they have satisfied the kirk for their scandall or have found caution to do soe.' Only with these precautions could one be certain that a woman hired as a wet nurse would not have abandoned her baby at someone's door or left it to be cared for by the parish. Clearly the writers of the petition, who planned the first authorized employment agency to be set up in Edinburgh, were aware that the old personal world where employers knew their servants and the background they came from, had gone.[7]

Enhancement of upper-class housing and comfort would take some time to affect the standard of living of the peasantry. True, it was peasant families that would provide the servants for the big house, and whose labour services would help to build the new mansion.[8] But the more sophisticated products that were taken for granted by the upper classes came from abroad. Elizabeth Mure of Caldwell points out that in the early decades of the eighteenth century the fine linen needed by young gentlemen for their shirts, and by the less delicate-minded older folk for the necks and sleeves of theirs, came from Holland, though ladies wore the country linen. In the 1730s there was a craze for the wearing of the native fine linen by gentle folk.[9] But the linen industry did not achieve a grand scale until the 1750s. One of the delaying factors was that the peasant economy was unable to provide tolerable quality: because this was taken for granted, nobody tried to encourage it to do so. It was a standing complaint that linen yarn spun by the ordinary Scottish housewife in the ordinary cottage could not afterwards be whitened to compete with Dutch thread.

When we look in detail at Scottish housing we can see plentiful reasons for the dirt that housewifely thumbs and fingers pressed into the yarn. In 1690 Sir John Clerk of Penicuik made a survey of the housing on his newly acquired estate of Loanhead and

Lasswade, reviewing his purchase as a merchant accustomed to stock-taking. There were 105 houses on the estate. Of these eight were fairly substantial, containing several rooms: four had at least one room with a glazed window, and five of them had a part of a second storey. To achieve such a development the ground floor would have had to have strong walls and ceilings finished, floors joisted, and of course there had to be some sort of a stair, probably a 'turnpike' or spiral staircase. Such solidity of construction would probably be accompanied by built-in chimneys, instead of mere holes in the roof. The eight bigger houses were for the aristocracy of the peasant community, six richer farmers, the brewer and the miller. Typical of them is one described as a 'fyne house': 'Thatched, two storie high, consisting of a large laigh hall with a large chimnie in the East gavel and of a laigh bed chamber with a chimnie, two windows, glass casements and stanchels in the laigh storie . . . with a timber scale stair with two bed chambers and two chimnies and a closet above, all well joisted and floored, in all five rooms.' (The closet, even though it was chimneyless and probably windowless counted as a room).

Then there were seven houses for the middling folk, the craftsmen, the officials of the mine, a merchant. The village lawyer for instance, had a living-room and a pantry. The remaining 90 houses were all one-roomed affairs, whether they stood in the village or on the farms, whether for peasant, schoolmaster of miners. The biggest measured 38 ft by 15 ft, the smallest 12 ft square. For the most part they were 20 ft by 15 ft, with no adornments; no glass for instance, though one or two had also a barn and one an outside oven. They rented at 4 or 6 pounds Scots a year, and had cost about 24 pounds to build. Glass at this date cost 4 pounds a square foot, which put it well beyond the means of the lesser folk. Instead they might have a wooden casement, and the richer ones would have had an iron latch on the door.[10]

So the bulk of the population lived in a house 20 ft by 15 ft, paying for it in rent or services. The village tailor paid in fish, 120 trout and 60 eels a year, the miners in coal. In this dusky, crowded space each family lived, cooked, made its own cheese, candles, cloth and leather, and perhaps its own beer. One of the rules of the local baron court was that pigs if kept, were to be kept indoors. If this was the housing of one of the richest parts of the country we do not need to look very far for an explanation of the poor quality of Scottish domestic products, the dirty and smelly linen, butter and cheese. Poverty is self-sustaining.

Dirt was, in fact, the usual thing that struck visitors to Scotland in the seventeenth and early eighteenth centuries. Perhaps one of the most convincing of these had been Sir William Brereton in 1635 whose diary returns again and again to the topic. Not only did he find the Scots dirty but also 'sluttish'. The houses in Edinburgh were filled with the effluvia of inadequate sanitary provision - a barrel in the basement. The use of stale urine as a bleaching agent, not properly washed out, made the linen stink. The pewter was not properly cleaned from one meal to the next. Women washed linen, when they did, by putting it in a big tub with water and treading it to work the dirt loose. Many male visitors noted this, with a pleasurable shock at the amount of female thigh disclosed. Brereton remarked that they gave up washing at a point when, to his eyes, they should have begun, but he was truthful enough to point out that the technique at least kept the legs and feet of the women clean.[11]

Dirt brings with it disease; overcrowding makes easy the exchange of disease. The reputation the Highlands had gained by mid-seventeenth century of a place where you were sure to catch the itch suggests at least that this particular infection which thrives on close contact cannot have been very common in the Lowlands. But parish registers of the early eighteenth century make frequent references to other diseases, killers, that spread in unhygienic conditions - fever, probably typhus, the bloody flux (dysentery), 'worm fever', 'bowel hive' or infant diarrhoea. The most serious burden that the squalor of poverty places on an undeveloped society is probably not so much the inability to produce desirable commodities for exchange, or to make the best uses of its resources in food, as the high level of ill health and death.

The work of the first demographer of Scotland, Dr Alexander Webster, gives us an age distribution of population for the mid-eighteenth century which implies an expectation of life of 28 years.[12] The few scraps of information we have for the seventeenth century give us no statistical reason to think it was higher then, and non-statistical reasons for thinking it lower. This means that the ordinary family was familiar with death, and in particular often experienced the loss of a parent. There is a list of the poor made in Yester parish, East Lothian, which shows that widows with young or fairly young children formed a large part of those unable to support themselves in bad times. A list of heads of families in Inverkeithing in 1752 shows us 8% headed by women; another for Abdie in 1751 gives 21%.[13] Of course many widows remarried. Still, the community was dragged down by a high burden of dependency resulting from the deaths of men in the prime of life.

Poverty also shows in the diet of common people. It is easy to forget the narrow range of foodstuffs available for most in the late seventeenth and early eighteenth centuries because we have detailed acounts of the splendid feasts of the rich. Sir John Gordon of Gordonstoun described the range of meat and fish available in the early seventeenth century in glowing terms.[14] Visitors who have left accounts were often less enthusiastic about the quality and choice available. Brereton in Carrick dined on what he thought a poor menu of oatcakes, eggs and buttered dried fish. He usually did better on the food side but often had only water to drink. We have a detailed account of what an upper-class family considered suitable for adolescent boys at college: three meals a day of generous quantities which included a quart of milk, with pottage, three quarters of a pound of oatcake, broth and boiled or roasted meat for dinner with the allowance of meat at half a leg of mutton each or a fowl, supper of three eggs, cheese and oatcake. The obvious gap in this diet is any trace of vegetable, and one is not entirely surprised that one of the boys suffered from long-standing sores in winter.[15] For the 1730s the Ochtertyre house book shows a landed family doing itself very well indeed, and even remedying this gap. Vegetables appear frequently, and even in mid-winter there were suppers of spinach and eggs. Presumably they had a hotbed in the garden.[16] This of course was part of the movement for more elegant and comfortable living, including the owning of gardens, in the central decades of the century. None of this has much relevance to the diet of the ordinary people, the peasant farmers, cottars and labourers.

Social historians find the diets of people on poor relief useful as a guide to the accepted lowest level of standards. In cases where the poor law was administered in poorhouses this may be an unreliable guide, for few institutions would actually feed people as badly as the poorest in the world outside might feed themselves. Also in institutions food will be given out separately to members of a family in proportions more equal than families in difficulties usually determine for themselves. In Scotland relatively few of the poor were in poorhouses, and where they were the house usually provided merely a roof; the poor sustained themselves on their own allowances in food or money. We can find enough references in session registers from lowland Scotland to see what was regarded as a 'norm' of diet for the poor, and in parishes in 'straitening circumstances' through poverty or dearth we can see even more clearly the concept of what was necessary for survival in hard times. The commonest allowance was a peck of oatmeal a week for an adult, which was also what could be bought with the gaol allowance for prisoners of 1s. Scots a day.[17] In times of dearth the gaol allowance went up to 2s. In the famine of the 1690s the parish of Chirnside, pensioning its paupers on to the various families of the parish, laid down that they were to receive 10s. Scots, or three quarters of a peck of meal or a peck of beans a week, survival rations, not adequate allowances. At the same period the parish of Spott was paying for the support of two small orphan girls a peck and a half of oatmeal a week and 40s. a quarter. This was more than a famine allowance and would leave something over for clothes and even for profit for looking after them, and since the little girls were too young to need three quarters of an adult's food, it is likely that some of the oatmeal was exchanged for other items, a little butter, milk and the occasional egg. At any rate the orphans survived for several years and were apprenticed out at the age of 11. In the case of long-term care of an adult, for instance of a lunatic, a parish would at intervals arrange for clothes, and would usually do something to keep the pauper in milk — it might for instance buy him a cow and rent grazing. This implies that milk and milk products were regarded as normal parts of the diet.[18]

How adequate were such diets? Oatmeal, stone ground as it would be, is a good basic food with a high cereal content for a grain. But unless the diet contains fats of some kind there would be deficiency of vitamins A and D; unless some of it was eaten raw or the diet supplemented by berries or kale, scurvy was likely, and in any case it would mean too little iron and calcium for health. With milk, butter and kale available, and most cottages kept a kale-yard, these weaknesses might well be overcome for an adult. 'Might' is the important word here. Recent work on nutrition has shown that it is not enough for a necessary ingredient to be available in food: some foodstuffs contain inhibitors which prevent the absorption of various chemicals, and the efficacy of such inhibitors, for instance phytic acid, varies according to the physiology of individuals and their past dietary habits. We are now alert to the likelihood of iron and calcium deficiencies in apparently healthy people. Work on Scottish diets of the 1790s and later, with regular but not large amounts of protein food and dairy produce, has shown them to be inadequate on any feasible division over the family as a whole.[19]

We are much less clear about what children ate than about their parents, for this depends on social assumptions that are rarely put into writing. Unless milk or cheese figured in the diet in large quantities, a diet based on oatmeal would certainly be short of calcium and protein. Probably many children had their growth held back by protein lack. There is no evidence to show that cheese occupied the position of the protein food in Scotland that it did in England. The horrifying impact of epidemics in the child population in the eighteenth century, for instance that of measles in Kilmarnock in 1752 which killed 54 children out of a total population of about 4,400 suggests malnutrition of this type.[20] But Kilmarnock was a partly urban parish with a population largely dependent on wages, and low wages at that. As far as the peasantry goes, most of them, as tenant farmers or hinds, would have had pasture for a cow or two, and kept hens to pay the rent, and, if tenants, might have the privilege every now and then of eating up old stock, sheep or ageing cattle. Various baron courts laid down that no more hens should be kept than were necessary for paying the rent, but such a regulation is inherently impractical. Altogether we should expect the rural population to be better supplied with protein foods than urban wage-earners.

Lowland Scotland is, as visitors pointed out, corn country. That is, cereals were the main production. But upland Scotland, the Highlands, Galloway, the Borders, relied more on pasture. The coasts are deeply indented, giving protected areas for fishing. Dunbar was a herring port, and the old tracks over the Lammermuirs record the routes by which herring passed inland. In most towns fresh fish was available. In all these areas diet with adequate protein was possible for those who could afford it or had the ownership of the means of getting it. McGuffog, for instance, had the skins of eight sheep that had died in the snow the previous winter and two cow hides undergoing treatment in his house. It is unlikely that the household had not had the meat to eat. He had five cows with calves, so milk was plentiful. Upland Scotland increased its grain supply by selling animals and animal produce to the plains. The impression we get from the forfeited estate accounts in the 1750s is that in many places the amount of surplus animal produce was very small indeed, but it may have been greater before the population rise of the eighteenth century.[21] The famous 'Whiggamore raid' of 1649 got its name from the regular Galloway cattle droves to the west for this purpose. We have minor local glimpses of special foods. There is the sudden increase in goat skins in the export figures of the 1690s; 100,000 of them, instead of the normal 50,000, in one year, showing that the highlanders were eating their last resort, their goat stock, in the famine.[22] The hill men of Galloway, says a description of the 1680s, had great guzzles on pickled eels and fermented whey in the winter. In Galloway and in the Highlands those along the shore fell back on cockles when all else failed.[23]

For both upland and lowland Scotland diet was, when adequate, often monotonous and not particularly palatable, though here upland fared better than lowland, for milk and cheese make oatmeal and bere meal slip down more easily. Neither oats nor bere will make a real bread. They were eaten as bannocks or oatcake, often baked on a hot stone if the household could not afford an iron girdle. Scotland, even in the mid-seventeenth century, was known as the 'land of cakes', i.e. a country where bread was not available. Oatmeal also makes porridge. An indication of the meagreness of the diet is the frequent reference to 'sowens'. This was a dish made by collecting the husks of oats after milling, and steeping them in water. After many days the residue of the meal in them clouded the water. It may also have fermented slightly. The water was strained off and boiled till it set into a slightly sour, viscous gel. It was considered a delicacy.

People living close to the threat of total failure of food supply are not particularly interested in variety in diet: reliability is of far greater significance. Here again the poverty of the country was a block to security. Harvest failure was a real risk all through the seventeenth century. Things improved after 1660, but the bad harvest of 1674 caused suffering, dislocation of the market and death in eastern Scotland. The great famine of 1696-9 lives on in the misleading phrase, for which there is no near-contemporary backing, of 'the seven ill years of King William's reign'. It was quite bad enough at four. The war created by the Revolution was already causing unemployment and consequently vagrancy when in 1695 the price of grain unexpectedly rose. Next year it was at famine level in the south, and after a brief respite due to a better harvest in 1697, there was a further disastrous failure of crops throughout the country in 1698. Even the apparently successful harvest of 1699, for which both government and church gave heartfelt thanks, did not bring down the price of grain, perhaps because all reserves had been used up. In some parts of the south-west shortages continued after the harvest of 1700.

The famine had struck when there were already signs of strain in the economy, and when social cohesion had been weakened in many areas, particularly the south, by the forcing out of episcopal ministers after the Revolution. In places forced to accept a new, and perhaps unpopular minister, the kirk session might be paralysed by bad relations between minister and elders, and with no active kirk session there would be no poor relief.

The story seems to have been one of a combination of late frosts, summer drought and a wintry September. Much of northern

Europe shared in one or other of the bad years, so that only small
quantities of high-priced food could be brought in. But even small
quantities can, and in many cases did, make the difference between
starvation and survival. The problem was the typical one of an
undeveloped economy, the lack of an effectively monetarized
society. People who normally raised their own food were competing
in a small market with the few who did not, and prices rose to levels
at which most had simply not the wealth to buy. Some died of
starvation directly, some of the epidemics that starvation brings, and
these epidemics would be carried from place to place by desperate
people looking for food or work. Sir Robert Sibbald, a sympathetic
and intelligent observer with a taste for natural history, wrote a little
book, for future reference, of what the poor might eat if such a
situation recurred. His recipes show what people could be reduced
to; boiled deer horn, the bark of trees, nettle soup. The list is long
and dismaying. Against his remark, 'all may see death in the faces
of the poor', should be set the most modern estimate of the deaths
caused directly or indirectly by the disaster — between 5 and 10% of
the total population.[24]

That it was not more can be attributed to two main factors. One
was that by the 1690s many parishes had organized a system of poor
relief that was at least enough to keep people alive. The scale of this
in a small community can be seen in one of these, Yester in East
Lothian. This parish may have had a population of something over
1,100. The list of people who received relief, often for a whole family
and usually on several occasions, numbers 121 names during the
whole decade of the 1690s. Even so it was only enabled to carry
through regular support by a loan from a neighbouring parish.[25] The
other saving factor was that epidemics did not easily march across a
countryside where the population lived in small hamlets and joint
farms rather than in nucleated villages. Even the most infectious of
the directly communicated diseases, smallpox, can be found in the
eighteenth century striking only one part of a dispersed parish on a
particular visitation. The dispersed pattern of local settlement,
which discouraged specialization in craft work and so was partly
responsible for poverty, did at least play a part in people's survival.

— Chapter 5 —

Money Moving

'The spirit of the age affects all the arts, and the minds of men being once roused from their lethargy, and put into a fermentation, turn themselves on all sides and carry improvements into every art and science.'

David Hume

I N 1708 there were 34 post offices in Scotland, in 1715 60, in 1741 over 100.[1] These figures give a measure of the early eighteenth-century expansion in amenity, particularly in amenity that deeply affected the middling ranks of society, both in their affairs, business and politics, and in their personal lives. A similar expansion took place in newspapers. There were no regular newspapers before the founding of the *Edinburgh Courant* in 1705, but in the 1720s this was joined by another newspaper in Edinburgh, the *Caledonian Mercury*, and after 1750 newspapers were founded in other towns, and the service expanded rapidly. By the 1770s every important town in Scotland had at least one newspaper publishing on several days a week.[2] These are minor signs of an important change in the country, the increased use and significance of money.

Some of this change came from direct increases in the efficiency of farming and in the scope of overseas trade. But a lot seems to have come from increased demand for goods and services. There had been nothing stopping farmer McGuffog[3] from selling a cow or two and using the money to buy a little more comfort; anything from a second candlestick to a second room to the house. It was, presumably, the force of convention, the fixed pattern of life, that kept him living so meanly, though meanness could, of course, be simple prudence; he might need all his stock to see him through a season of starvation, a natural or man-made disaster. But by 1740 people with much less in the way of real wealth than McGuffog will be found indulging in comforts, in better furniture, in more space, in a wider range of cookery utensils and so in a more varied diet, and in particular in cleanliness. The most striking change in people's possessions is in the stocks of linen that were being built up. Cleanliness can either be achieved by relatively expensive domestic equipment, for instance today by washing machines and tumble dryers, in the eighteenth century by building chimneys into the walls so that rooms ceased to be full of soot, or else by a big reserve of changes of linen. Without a proper chimney, washing clothes will not get them white in winter if they have to be dried in a single-roomed house full of smoke and smuts. In any case life in such a room becomes so intolerable when it is full of damp sheeting that most people will prefer dirt. Dirty linen in unimproved housing has to be stockpiled till summer, when it can be both washed outside and 'booked' or bleached in the sun. If a household is to be able to put off washing day for six months and yet to enjoy clean linen reasonably often, it needs very large stocks. Linen stocks become a sign of respectability, and this ensures that they stay large even after swifter washing becomes feasible. In the 1770s we can

12   David Allan's representation of the annual catechizing of a parish by the minister in the eighteenth century. There is obviously some last minute revision going on

13   The procession for the opening of the General Assembly moves up the High Street of Edinburgh, 1793

14 A lowland wedding, 1684, painted by the Dutch artist De Wit

15 Market day in Campbeltown, late eighteenth century

16 By the late eighteenth century the Highlands were regarded as romantic, and tartan was part of that romance. Here the Duke of Atholl poses with his family, with Blair Castle in the background

17 Craftsmen working on repairs to Holyrood House in 1721, with their tools. From the left: sieve wright, slater, glazier, cooper, mason wright, bow-maker, painter, plumber and upholsterer

18 A golfing portrait, from the late eighteenth century, of William Inglis. Golf, then as now, was a sport for all classes, even for the fisherwives of Musselburgh

19　Planting potatoes in Skye, late nineteenth century. The foot plough which the man is using enabled very small patches of soil to be cultivated

20　Shooting in the Highlands in the late nineteenth century

21 The tower-house of Craigievar, completed in 1626. This is the most impressive of the tower-houses of the north-east because the owners could never afford to modify or enlarge it in safer times. Such a house was not easily broken into by marauding bands, though it would not withstand a serious siege

22 Inside a seventeenth-century tower-house. The long gallery at
Crathes Castle

23 The elegance and comfort of eighteenth-century aristocratic life: the library at Mellerstain, probably the most beautiful of the great Scottish houses, designed by Robert Adam

24 The south front at Mellerstain: formal gardening and a nostalgic use of castellation

find a minor highland tacksman, William MacIntosh of Balnespick, making a note that he possessed 32 shirts and 'all the night shirts I have is only 20 and one useless'.[4] These items were not for conspicuous consumption, but simply the large stock necessary for a change of clothes once a week.

Linen, letters, newspapers, were all things that a large number of people wanted to spend money on. Better housing, which was also an eighteenth-century taste for at least the middling ranks and higher, brought with it the need for more furniture, and some of this would be made of imported woods, rosewood or mahogany.[5] Hardwoods such as these and the native oak require more skill and better tools in the making than had the native pine or the imported fir and spruce which had been the mainstay of furnishings in the past. Expanding minor industries met other expanding needs, such as writing paper, sugar and tobacco. A significant change in diet in the eighteenth century was the introduction of new beverages. Coffee led to the creation of coffee houses in the towns, where men met and talked and did business. The clubs and societies which were a vital part of the intellectual life of Edinburgh made use of these. Tea was of even greater significance. It was regarded as the sphere of the housewife, and brought with it an element of ritual. You did not drink it out of pewter, and indeed the flavour of the tea of this period, when it came from China, would probably have been spoilt by the use of half-clean pewter. You had a special set of china or earthenware, tea pot, cups and 'sasers', a slop-bowl, and, if possible, silver spoons. This was all kept in the best room of the house, usually in a locked cupboard. Tea in 1700 was very expensive, costing over £1 sterling per pound. In the 1720s it was still out of reach of most. The accounts of the Lochs of Drylaw give prices of 10 to 16 shillings,[6] but a good part of this was duty. By the 1740s smugglers were providing tea for about 3s. a pound. Smuggling was big business and in touch with all markets. Tea had thus come within the financial reach of ordinary labourers. Even while expensive it had been spreading to working families in Edinburgh. In the 1740s Duncan Forbes, Lord Advocate, alarmed for the receipts of the excise on malt, attempted to confine the use of tea to landowning families, by means of licences.[7] The scheme was a survival of the old idea of sumptuary legislation: that each rank in society had a pattern of expenditure beyond which it should be legally prevented from going. Forbes would have been too late with his scheme, if he had ever been allowed to put it into action, as a run-through of the surviving inventories of the merchant and artisan classes in Edinburgh from

1720-41 shows.[8] Not all these inventories show households which had already invested in the equipment for tea-making, but many had, almost as many as had also taken to the equally newfangled idea of not eating with your fingers.

The use of fingers should not be taken as a sign of lack of fastidiousness: houses were much more generously supplied with table linen than today, and people were expected to use table cloths or 'servits' (napkins) to wipe their hands on. Forks are not necessary for a diet of oatcake and porridge, and most households were well supplied with horn spoons. Meat eating, for which forks are useful, was a sign of middling rank. Working families might have a meat meal only a few times in the year, even though a move from a cereal diet to one with meat was not very expensive. (The ration of meat prices to cereals was four to one or five to one instead of the ten or twelve to one it is today.) Alexander Cowie, a journeyman wigmaker, is a sample of a working man: at his death in 1741 he had no forks and no tea-making equipment. Alexander Swinton, a clerk in the Canongate in 1732, had no knives or forks, but he had a copper tea kettle, a stoneware tea pot and two blue and white china dishes to drink out of. Margaret Johnston, the widow of an Edinburgh merchant, had in 1741 a coffee roaster and an iron coffee pot, a tea kettle, four tea pots (three of them broken), five saucers and eight cups (and clearly needed to teach her servants how to wash up carefully). Archibald Cameron, landwaiter at Leith, (a lower middle-class official position) had a tea table, 12 cups and saucers, but no knives or forks in 1741. A ban on tea for people such as these would have been unenforceable without intrusive policing. But outside Edinburgh tea was still the privilege of the upper classes. As the century wore on tea became the normal luxury for all 'middling' types of people, and the standard luxury of urban labourers. It created a new social pattern and time of day: 'afternoon tea' was what the Reverend John Mill from Shetland took when visiting the wife of a fellow minister in South Leith in 1754.[9]

Tea was only one, but the easiest for the historian to trace, of the increasing number of things that money could buy, and its spread symbolizes the increasing importance of money. One of the signs of this was the movement in 1750-1 in the General Assembly to get the stipends of ministers increased. The church argued that the cost of living was higher than it had been at the start of the century. This was onlly partly true. The price of the basic cereals, bere and oatmeal, had changed very little, though wheat prices had risen considerably. Beer and salt, both fundamental items of diet, now bore tax, and that on salt was particularly heavy. Cattle prices had begun to rise in the

1740s, which would mean that meat, dripping, dairy produce and candles now cost more. If a minister was prepared to live on oatcake and porridge with a little butter and cheese, and only a small amount of beer, the main added expense would probably have been a slight rise in the acceptable wages of his servants. Wheaten bread was little used outside the ranks of gentry and merchants. Many of the middle-class extras that were necessary to such people's way of life, pots and pans, good quality cloth and fine linen, writing paper and books, medicaments (mostly purges) and china or earthenware were easier to obtain than they had been and cheaper, even though a lot of these still had to be brought in by ship from England. Good furniture, tobacco, tea and coffee, fluffy English blankets, wall hangings: these goods were increasingly bought and mark a new level of comfortable living. A middling rank family would expect to have mats on the floor in its house, it might even in a town have curtains at the windows; it would expect more house room than in the past, three or four rooms, or if in the country a tidy Georgian house with glazed windows. Increasingly the urban middling ranks took to using coal, not just in Edinburgh where they had long done so, but in towns not on the coal measures. Coal had to be paid for, whereas peat for a peat fire merely meant sending people to cut peats in the town's moss. By the end of the century gentry in the country were using coal if transport was not prohibitively expensive, whereas in the earlier decades they had regarded the obligation to bring in peats as one of the most important of the services laid on their tenantry. Almost every inventory of possessions by the year 1750 includes a looking-glass. Even Alexander Cowie had one. A middling rank family might have two or three, not just sources of personal gratification but a sign of attention to the outward appearance. Another significant change in customs would be the use of individual drinking glasses. In a book of etiquette of 1720 [10] the passing of the glass from one to another was still taken for granted (nice-mannered people refrain from breathing out into the wine and clouding it before passing it on). But by 1740 a household with pretensions to gentility would be provided with more than one goblet. A further source of expenditure was also the cause of a good deal of indignant writing by political economists. This was the use of English blankets rather than the local produce. English blankets were soft and fluffy and would wear out after a mere 20 years or so of use, whereas the Scotch blanket was almost indestructible and mortified the flesh by its scratchiness. English blankets, significantly confined usually to the bed of the householder, are a regular feature of mid-century inventories, in spite of the denunciations of moralists and political economists.

So even if the prices of necessities had not risen much, and those of luxuries were falling, there is ample evidence as to why ministers were feeling the pinch by mid-century. Schoolmasters also were under financial pressure to put on classes that would bring in extra fees. The pressure was to get worse, for in the second part of the century began a steady rise in grain prices, which though it meant bigger stipends (for the stipend was calculated in grain) meant that everything was likely to cost more.

The ministers did not get their rise in 1751. They were defeated by the sharp practice of the landowners, who as elders took an equal part in the General Assembly but also as freeholders and Members of Parliament were able to resist in one capacity what they appeared to support in another. The care of landowners for their revenue which this displays was not new: on all occasions the landowning class can be found resisting having any regular charges laid on their estates, even if personally they might be generous to good causes. But already by mid-century some landowners had begun to feel that the level of their revenues was not immutable and might be enhanced. The 2nd Duke of Argyll had been an early example of this by trying to introduce competitive bidding for leases in Tiree, and some of the estates forfeited after the 1745 rebellion, those near the Highland line, can be seen to have undergone some reorganization aimed at a higher rental.[11] There were other ways in which the return of land could be increased. Some landowners were showing an increased interest in mining and in rural industry. The word 'improve', which was becoming fashionable, has its ambiguities. To the real 'improver' it meant to develop: to exploit more intensively and efficiently the resources of an estate, to reorganize production, and to invest capital in the expectation of higher yields. But it could also be used to refer to an 'improved' rent, and in this sense meant merely raised. This form of improvement could not for long take place without the other, but not all landowners recognized this fact.

Pressure by the landed classes for more money could be both a burden and a benefit to society, and this pressure was to increase as, after 1750, the growth of population forced up the price of the basic cereals. Landowners, still in most cases receiving rents in kind, were sensitive to the change in market values. The new idea, that landed income could change, would spread more rapidly when the facts were forced home in practice. A late eighteenth-century landowner could not but be acquainted with the idea of improvement. Reorganization and investment meant that it was advantageous to have measures of the extent and quality of the land, so there developed openings for surveyors and agricultural advisers. New crops might be grown, trees would be needed for hedging and for orchards, and so we find seeds-men setting up shops in the cities and advertisements in the news-papers of young trees for sale.[12] The landowner would use his authority over his tenants to drive them into accepting reorganization and the use of new methods. The hardest thing, said Sir John Clerk of Penicuik, was to get his tenants to accept the reorganization of the joint farm of Penicuik into separate holdings, though much of the Lothians had been in separate farms even in the seventeenth century.[13] The most famous early improver was, of course, Cockburn of Ormiston, and his letters to his gardener give us an insight into the pressures that had to be used. We can see Cockburn scolding the man into compliance. 'Don't fall into the stupid sleepy way so common in Scotland. Get the best plants and Seeds you now can . . .' 'Could the Lasie man bring himself to more activity or the Covetous man to a larger way of thinking, they would both get more business and more money from having more customers.' 'Do you think it possible that there are not Families and Taverns in Eden that would give reasonably for young pease and Beans in July and August if they could get them . . . It is the not being able to get good things which makes people not have them.'[14] The history of later development shows that Cockburn was right. Desire for gain, followed intel-ligently, could have social advantages. So could the desire of the aristocracy for a higher standard of living. The great country house of the eighteenth century was a focus for the use of skill: the building, particularly in details such as doors, windows, plasterwork and roofing, needed skilled workers, and though at first many of these workers would have to be brought in from a distance, even from abroad, eventually native carpenters and plasterers did the work. Then there was the need for fine furnishings.

Equally important was the fact that the big house recruited and trained servants to standards acceptable to the upper class, and the point most rigorously insisted on was cleanliness. It was not merely that gentry preferred their own persons and clothes clean — Boswell's diary, for instance, shows that he was accustomed to clean linen every day, at least when in town[15] — but that they recognized that this meant that the whole house had to be free from vermin and dirt. 'You must keep youself very clean' runs the instruction of Lady Grisell Baillie to her butler, after detailed instructions about the cleaning of silver and bottles. The turnover of servants was continual. Of course some left at once, as the note by Lady Grisell about a cook's wages show: 'she staid only a night'. In 1715 there are notes which imply trouble in Lady Grisell's kitchen: 'Jean Hasnen came to be cook... to her for 2 Monethes caried away by constables L.1. 7.4., to Marie Swan cook for a week...'[16] But in any case most girls entering service, and many men too, did not intend to stay there for their lives. They would leave and marry after a few years. Their time in service would furnish savings, useful for setting up their own homes, and a taste for different patterns of living. Service might have introduced them to tea drinking, and almost certainly if in a big house, to the expectation of meat in their diet. It would certainly have shown them a higher level of cleanliness than that familiar at home, and since cleanliness is a comfort attractive to most people over the age of ten or so, as much of it as was practicable in a cottage would stay with them as a habit. At any rate it is in the 1770s that we have the first visitor from England to Scotland prepared to praise the standard of cleanliness of the homes of the common people — Thomas Bewick, with an artist's eye, who came from Newcastle to Scotland on a long tour in 1776 to mark the end of his apprenticeship.[17]

The most general source of increased wealth for landowners was agricultural reorganization, the so-called agricultural revolution. Though there are instances of new agricultural methods in the first half of the eighteenth century, the main development was after 1760; in northern areas such as Aberdeenshire little large-scale change happened before the early years of the nineteenth century, and in some parts of the Highlands farming is still not reorganized. The impact of the new farming on society was profound. First of all it provided new or better crops. The potato is the single most important innovation in basic diet between 1600 and 1800. Its use seems to have spread across Scotland from south-west to north-east between 1750 and 1780. By the latter year it was rare to find a place in which it was not a regular field crop. It helped, particularly in the Highlands, to reduce the risk of starvation from harvest failure, though in the most serious harvest failure of the later eighteenth century, that of 1782, it was social organization, the working of poor relief and government aid, rather than the potato (which was hit by early frosts that year) that saved the situation.

The most characteristic product of the new farming was improved winter feed for cattle. This meant a great step forward in productivity. Cattle could be kept in milk through the winter, and did not have to spend the first two months of the summer recuperating from semi-starvation. The crops for this winter feed were labour intensive, particularly the turnip which would be the favoured crop on the lighter soils, and which involved sowing, hoeing and lifting.

T.C. Smout has noted the relationship between turnip-growing and a sustained demand for agricultural labour in the Lothians at the end of the eighteenth century.[18]

The new unit of farming was the separated farm, its boundaries 'enclosed', i.e. fenced, and further hedges or walls erected to separate fields from one another. These farms were of varying size, but almost everywhere there would be fewer of the new farms than there had been tenant farmers in the old joint farms. The whole system of joint farming had to go. Improved implements and soil in better condition meant that fewer oxen or horses were necessary to draw the plough, but even so many of the old tenantry did not individually own a plough team. So divisions in the ranks of the peasantry become sharper. Some become farmers under the new dispensation, in some cases managing farms much bigger than they had known before. A farm of 200 acres would not be abnormal, though in the eighteenth century 120 acres remained a more common size, and its rent required the farming to be carried on skilfully and with an eye to the market. The rent would be in money, not in kind. New farmhouses would be built, of six or eight rooms, and new farm buildings, and the farm would also carry cottages for the married labourers or hinds. These, though small by modern standards, would probably be better built than most of those in the list recorded by Clerk of Penicuik in 1680.[19]

Even before full development hard work had been the order of the day in the Lothians. George Robertson has described the pattern of the old farming before 1765 in a book, *Rural Recollections*, which has rightly become a classic. Some of this hard work came from inefficiency. 'Nothing was put upon a cart, that could be carried on a horse. Corn and meal, of all kinds, were generally conveyed on horseback, in sacks...' He describes the common type of Lothian farm as of one to three ploughgates, that is 60-180 acres, using both hinds, that is married labourers living in their own cottages and paid largely in produce, and unmarried farm servants living in the two-roomed farmhouse. The cottages were 'very mean hovels', often without a chimney still, which tells one a lot about the ramshackle nature of their construction. There would be two maidservants on the farm. Each week one of these would spin the whole time, except when she helped with the milking. The other was the 'scodgie' or maid of all work. 'She had to cook the victual; make up the beds; keep the fire in order; bring in the water; wash the tables and dishes; sweep the house; and, twice or thrice a week, kirn the milk. In short she did everything,; and, if all that is stated was not enough, she had to assist in milking the cows; and, that no idle

time should be left her, she too had her spinning-wheel, at which it
was expected that she would make out her *hesp* of yarn in the week;
whilst the other lass had to make one out every day'.[20] The two girls
would change over each week. I don't know which workload
sounds the more gruelling.

Robertson is giving us the picture of the larger farms in the most
advanced part of Scotland, often already separate units even if not
using the new crops. For the most part the units were smaller, the
structure simpler. We can see that this must have been so from
parish lists of householders. In Dairsie (Fife) in 1747 there were 51
cottars to 34 'tenants and tradesmen', and the tradesmen, men such
as the smith, miller and wright, would still farm as well as work at
their trade. Barr (Ayrshire) in 1745 had 81 cottars to 31 tenants.
Roberton in Lanarkshire in 1747, 37 cottars to 43 tenants.[21] In these
glimpses of the two ranks, Barr, the parish most generously
provided with cottars, had fewer than three cottars to each tenant,
so that there cannot have been much in the way of a farm hierarchy.
The farmer would have men working under him, adding to the yield
of their cottar holding by labour, but probably not working for him
full-time, and he himself would be working in the field with them.
But under the new system the farmer would become more clearly the
supervisor, though in upland areas small farms, where he would
have little extra labour, continued more successfully than in the
main corn-growing plains. For Fife in 1800 we have this picture:
'Formerly it was customary for the farmers to subject themselves to
every kind of drudgery and hard labour, undergoing the same toil,
living upon the same fire, and often eating at the same table with
their servants. And in some instances this may be the case still . . . But
many of the farmers now occupy a more respectable and important
station. Their chief business is to superintend. The operative and
servile part is committed to others . . .'[22] The writer adds that 'the
apartments' of the farmhouse are so arranged and the general
economy is regulated 'to produce a more marked distinction between
master and servant, and to put an end to that indiscriminate
intercourse in respect of sitting and eating, which was common in
former times'. Even bearing in mind the fact that 'respectable' had a
different shade of meaning then from what it bears today, there is
discernible a note of approval of the new arrangements by the writer.

Larger farms meant fewer farmers. Better farming in larger units
meant more farm capital. Not only was the new farmer separating
himself off from his farm servants; his relative wealth made a gulf
between them which it was unlikely that any worker would pass. It
became rare for a farm servant to be able to save enough to stock

even a small farm. The wages mentioned in the authority just quoted for the married farm servant (largely in kind), were worth £16 to £18 a year, for the unmarried living with the farmer, £8 to £12 in cash. The social separation was most acute in parts of eastern Scotland where farmers created the 'bothy system' of housing their work force. Bothies were dormitory houses for the unmarried labourers, where they slept and ate and cared for themselves, occasionally having cooking or cleaning done for them by one of the maids. Bothy culture developed its own ethos, a pattern of living which made saving difficult in a convivial and fairly brutal society.

So we get social divisions, temporary or permanent, sharpening into class. The new gulf would divide those of the old tenants who remained as farmers from those who had been turned into labourers. Both groups would have less contact with their land-owner than in the past. The new farms were paid for by money rents, though some services, particularly thirlage (which was legally difficult to get rid of) hung on into the nineteenth century.[23] This change had been urged by agricultural reformers for some time. George Dempster expressed himself on it in an imaginary address to landowners: 'Our Farmers want Capital and Skill. You Gentlemen will be great gainers by giving them both ... give them in the first place all their own. Give them their Time, give them their Labour and that of their Cattle and Horses and Servants, for at present you rob them of all. When they should be driving manure to their own Farms and fallowing their Grounds you employ them in digging your Peats ... When their own Corn is ripe for the Hook you require them to cut down yours. When they should be at market about their own business you require them to run your Errands ...'[24] It is worth noting that like many oppressed people given liberty, farmers freed from services took care to extract additional services from their own labourers. It was normal in the Borders, for instance, for hinds to have to provide a bondager, a female farm labourer, or to house one for the farmer.

Certainly services must have been an incumbrance to an active and ambitious tenant, though they provided a setting for idleness for others. Elizabeth Grant of Rothiemurchus recalls that ' an errand was a day's work, whether it took the day or only an hour or two.'[25] But services and rents paid in kind kept the different sections of rural society in constant contact. 'He paid 10 pounds to my wife (two bullocks)' is a typical entry in the early eighteenth-century rentals of Clerk of Penicuik, as evidence of this. Another even more vivid picture we have of the old unreformed agriculture is of the small highland tacksman out in the field with his tenants to get the harvest in, noting the composite crops that went into each stack, lending his tenantry money and tools in emergencies, and buying in food for them in time of shortage.[26]

The new agriculture gave more opportunity to the able and hard working, but, because it did so, showed up more sharply the inefficient. Once it was recognized that rent rolls were not immutably fixed, it became apparent that the yield on a landowner's capital was increased by efficient tenants. It would go harder for those who, through chance or necessity, were inefficient. In 1704 Sir John Clerk of Penicuik had faced a decision about the re-letting of one of his farms to a family of orphans. Alexander Livingstone and his wife had died, leaving a considerable debt and several children, the eldest boy, Robert, being 16. Against his judgment Sir John acquiesced in the renewal of the tenancy in the boy's name. His sister, Elspie, aged 18, would keep house for the family: uncles, also on the estate, would give advice. So would Sir John, and indeed he records on several occasions that he had done so. The farm servants were both 'honest and diligent'. Probably the land was not well cared for over the next few years, but the family could keep its head above water.[27] That sort of arrangement became unlikely under the new system. Families of this kind would have become labourers rather than tenants, and so be forced into poverty. The advantages that the new type of farming brought, and the variety of employments opening in a more lively economy, must be balanced against the new pressures produced and the tendency to sharpened social divisions between the 'comfortable' peasantry, the labourers and the poor.

This is not to say that within these groups people were worse off than before. The real income of a labourer, no less than of a tenant, rose in the eighteenth century. He had more money, and in possessions more wealth. Wages went up faster than the price of basic foods, except for individual years in the inflationary 1790s, and other prices tended to fall. There was more to spend money on. His diet by the 1780s had been widened; in some places he had begun to drink tea, and almost everywhere he now consumed potatoes and whisky. Potatoes in a moderate amount improve diet, reducing the risk of scurvy. Whisky seems to have fewer advantages, except palatability and immediate pleasure, and the change to it from beer as the main form of alcohol consumed in Scotland met then, and has met since, with criticism from all types of observer. It provided less in nutrients than does beer, and a far more rapid route to oblivion and alcoholism. Like all northern peoples the Scots have long had a reputation for hard and indiscriminate drinking, and there are numerous stories of accidental death from drunkenness to illustrate this. One of the main results of increased income was to make drunkenness possible more often. Alcohol, then as now, was involved in a structure of social occasions, ritual or orgy, and the relative smallness of whisky bottles and flasks enabled this to spread over outdoor activities. There were, however, other changes in the way of life that were indubitably improvements: more linen and household goods, better constructed houses, more fuel, cheaper pewter and pottery.

It was not only in agriculture that development and change were happening. The new or expanding industries meant more paid employment. They also meant more destitution and unemployment when a slump hit. The cut-back in the linen industry in the 1750s, when the government subsidy on export stopped, sent many of the weavers into the army,[28] the most despised and hated of occupations. Changes in the industrial pattern weakened the old church discipline. It became less possible for a kirk session to insist on a testimonial when a family moved into the parish. In any case the recognized existence of dissent within the presbyterian fold from the 1730s on meant that membership of a congregation and residence within a parish were not synonymous. But in practice most clergy continued to regard the entire protestant population of a parish as under their care, even if a proportion was known to belong to other congregations.[29] The dissenting churches grew most rapidly in the central and western sector of the central valley, in Glasgow, Stirlingshire and Fife, all areas of lively industry. At the same time that agricultural change was setting the tenantry free, at a price, the economy was weakening the bonds of church and society elsewhere.

Increased secularization is also shown in changes that came over the system of poor relief. In southern Scotland there developed a desire among landed society to organize this efficiently. One strand of this desire was a genuine current of humanitarianism, another a feeling for order and system in what was a part of public polity. There also seems to have been a simple desire for power. To some it was ridiculous that an important area of law and social control should be left to the individual initiatives of the various kirk sessions. The poor law policy of a parish necessarily affected other parishes. Some landowners felt that it was dangerous that considerable sums of money, in some cases left as legacies, should be controlled, and even actually held at home, by parish treasurers who were men of no social standing or education, and almost inevitably not owners of land. So we get two changes being effected in the poor law in the central decades of the eighteenth century. One was an attempt to put things on a larger and more regular basis, usually that of a county. Poorhouses, workhouses or orphanages should be built; they should be used to house the poor without allowing begging, they should be supported by church collections and legacies, by the products of the labour of the poor, and, as a reserve, by some sort of rate levied on the parishes using them. Various towns, for instance Edinburgh and Paisley, founded 'charity workhouses' on this sort of plan, but it also extended to rural areas. The Stewartry of Kirkcudbright, for instance, was attempting to rationalize relief and get rid of public begging as early as the 1720s. Many counties put forward plans to this effect later and some went some way in carrying them out. The reason why more did not can be seen in the problems that afflicted those that did. Parishes that made use of the schemes found that with the poor out of sight, church collections fell off. The constant badgering by beggars had anyway meant that a good deal of the cost of keeping the poor alive came not through the parish but in individual alms, and these disappeared now. As a result rates for poor relief were inescapable, and once a parish was rated church collections fell even lower. It then looked as if the new policy was going to saddle the parishes concerned perpetually with rates, and that the poor had become more expensive: assessment, it would be claimed, was encouraging pauperism. Rural parishes would withdraw from the scheme. In the towns, where this was not really practicable, the institutions for the poor would struggle on, trying to wrestle with the problem that once the poor are tucked away in poorhouses the charitable impulses of the public tend to dry up.

There is no doubt that poor rates, where a parish could be induced to undertake them, were a more reliable way of dealing with destitution than church collections, and in many cases the landowners, who organized the collection and administration of rates, were prepared to recognize social obligations. Tranent, a parish which had been under prosecution by the Lord Advocate in 1700 for failure to work the poor law properly in the recent famine, can be found undertaking a rating system conscientiously at the order of the sheriff in 1745.[30] In the crisis of the 1690s the performance of the parishes in relief had been very uneven. Where they had conscientiously tried to work the poor law it seems that the famine struck less devastatingly. In the same way the improved general organization of relief of the mid-eighteenth century had a lot to do with the fact that the severe food shortages of the century, those of 1740, 1782-3 and 1799-1800, did not have any drastic effect on population growth.

But the new lay feeling in society was not only a demand for efficiency; it was a demand for power. Many parishes, in the relatively easy circumstances of the mid-eighteenth century, free from famine, under relatively light impact of epidemic disease and before the slumps and booms of an industrialized economy, could manage to support their poor on purely voluntary funds, particularly if they had a few legacies. In the years 1747-51 we can see a series of quarrels in such parishes where landowners objected to the handling of large legacies or other funds by poorly educated elders, against whom, it was alleged, there could be no security since such men possessed no landed property. Cases of embezzlement could happen and certainly did — a particularly extensive structure of misappropriation of funds was revealed at Penninghame in 1732[31] — but the disputes which went to court in these years were exacerbated not by actual criminality but by personal tensions, religious schism and by the sheer bulk of the funds at issue. An example of this is Cambuslang. This parish had been the scene of a remarkable evangelical revival in 1742, in which many people at outdoor prayer meetings had experienced dramatic conversions. Outdoor meetings to commemorate and continue the 'great wark' of Cambuslang continued to he held yearly, producing repentance and a sense of union with God. People flocked to these occasions from many parts of Scotland, and were generous contributors at them. The funds of the parish swelled, even though much of the money was used in the organization of the great congregations and communions. One of the principal landowners was antagonized by the outdoor meetings: they damaged his fencing and, in his opinion, were a 'discredit to religion'. Accusations were made that the session did not keep proper accounts of its wealth, and was using the money, given for poor relief, for other purposes. The session countered with accusations that he was a dissenter and had been dilatory in handing over a legacy left to it by a relative.[32] What the legal dispute reveals is a cleavage in the community between two concepts of the roles of religion, of society and of wealth.

The outbreak of quarrels led to a series of judicial decisions. We should not be surprised that the lawyers and judges of the Court of Session should share the prejudices and beliefs of the landowners, for such they were themselves. They gave the landowners of a parish a right to share in the control of all the parish funds, from whatever source. This meant that a parishioner, contributing money at a church collection, would be handing it over to control by people who might in no real sense be part of the local community. Landowners might reside elsewhere, or belong to the episcopalian church, but they still controlled the use of all parish funds. The parish as a true community was already divided, and the new rulings accentuated the divisions.

Control by landowners of the money of a parish led to a basic change in the accepted poor law. It was a time of expanding opportunities; new types of work were available, the spectre of famine moved away. It became easy to ignore the fact that unemployment might exist, or that the wages of a labourer might be too low or too occasional to support his family. By the 1780s a new interpretation of the law was gaining acceptance, that poor relief was only for those incapacitated permanently from earning their living, and that even for these it should not be enough to live on. The pauper should supplement the aid from the parish by whatever he could extract from relatives and neighbours, usually, though those who accepted this interpretation of the law covered this up by more elegant language, by begging. The only temporary incapacity generally, though not universally, considered enough to justify poor relief was that of young children. This became the accepted form of the Scottish poor law, and much legal ingenuity was devoted to showing that this was the intention of its founding statutes. Even more than control by the landowners, this marked the breakdown of the parish community. To a needy man the kirk session had become a 'them', a representative of civil government, allotting him, if he qualified under the new rigorous rules, a small sum from either rates or collections, and leaving him to gather from his real community, his immediate friends or kindred, the real charity that would enable him to survive. Almost at the same time that the Scottish poor law became generally effective, it ceased to be the organ of a real sense of community.

So far this chapter has concentrated on the increase of wealth and economic activity in the Lowlands. In the Highlands the changes of the central decades of the eighteenth century were still more marked, for they were the result not only of economic change but of government policy and demographic pressure. The government, which could have done this earlier, pursued a policy after the defeat of the 1745 rebellion which was both an attack on aspects of highland culture and a limitation of the privileges or rights of some landowners and chiefs. Only a small part of the Highlands had been involved in the rebellion, but the opportunity was taken to alter basically civil and legal relationships within the whole highland area. The country was disarmed, and the wearing of highland dress made illegal. Cattle thieving, intimidation and murder as a method of discipline within the clan were put down in a campaign for law and order. Private feudal jurisdictions were bought up. The estates of those who had engaged in rebellion were handed over to commissioners who set out to organize them as model communities, areas of economic and social progress, while exile of the chiefs weakened the personal bond of clanship. The church was at last able to organize an effective presbyterian ministry in the area, and church and government together went on with a policy, which had started some 20 years earlier, of founding schools. There were parish schools, and extra charity schools for the vast parishes, and spinning schools. The aim was the establishment of habits of regularity, industry, literacy, the use of English and acceptance of the protestant religion. The ethos that was producing economic change in the Lowlands was to be transported to the Highlands. We might compare the enthusiastic comment of a visitor to Ormiston in the 1730s, 'thers not a boy or a girel of 7 years old but has something to do that ye will not see ane in the toun except in ane hour of play'[33] with the complaint of a factor for the forfeited estates in 1755 about Crieff, that there were 'crowds of little girls here that stroll about the streets playing at handball'.[34]

What lowland society and the government were expecting of highland society was that it should accomplish in a generation not only the cultural and linguistic assimilation that it had been resisting for centuries, but also the achievements of lowland Scotland of the past century and a half: the establishment of law and order, a new relationship of citizen to government, the acceptance of protestantism, the drive for self-education and the acceptance of money as a motive for action and a key to relationships. Some of these requirements were met, in particular the establishment of law and order. Highlanders settled down to be peaceable with an alacrity which gives considerable substance to the claim made by legal and governmental society earlier in the century that the power of chiefs to call out their men of war was an oppression.[35] Despite the much publicised 'Appin murder' of 1752, the shooting of a government servant on an unpopular task of rent collecting, there was little violence except in the immediate aftermath of the rebellion, and in the 1750s and 1760s the factors for the Forfeited Estates invariably report that all is quiet. In the 1770s, when Edinburgh and Glasgow organized subscriptions for the prosecution of offenders,[36] and their newspapers recorded some horrifying crimes in the rural areas of the Lowlands as well as in the cities, it was possible for tourists such as Boswell and Dr Johnson to explore the Highlands in safety. Even in the disturbances produced by the widespread opposition to the economic policies of highland landowners in the nineteenth century, the violence shown

by the peasantry was moderate and mostly of a ritual nature. It usually took the form of demonstrations in which women played the
leading role, and was usually defensive in purpose.[37] Those who
know the reputation of the different Scottish regiments in peace
time, either at home or in occupied territory, will be aware that even
in the twentieth century highland troops have been associated with
much less roughness and disorder than lowland.

Highlanders seem to have abandoned the old claims of chieftainship with little pain. This was partly because the chiefs were
themselves abandoning their obligations. That a chief should be the
father of his people had been interpreted, complained the 3rd Duke
of Argyll in 1743, that cheating was a thing 'in the Highlands they
think fair to do to their cheifs',[38] and this position ceased to suit the
chiefs as they came more and more to regard themselves as landowners with some additional advantages. Among these was the ability, profitable and prestigious, to raise regiments for the crown. But
men who came forward to serve in such regiments in the wars of the
French Revolution and after were usually impelled to this by the
economic needs of their parents. They served in return for explicit or
implicit bargains that their parents would continue to enjoy a croft,
or that there would be one for them on disbandment. Landowners
were still sufficiently fathers of their people to support them
through the potato famine in the mid-nineteenth century, but
increasingly in the eighteenth and nineteenth centuries absenteeism
by the great landowners whittled away their ability to lead highland
society, and the great landowners and the lesser aristocracy of the
Highlands, the tacksmen, were forced out by economic failure or by
the deliberate policy of their superiors. Chieftainship remained a sentimental notion for highlanders who had left the Highlands, but had
less and less reality at home. In this process the events of the rebellion of 1745 and its defeat, leading to forfeitures and exile, made
merely one big step in a staircase of decline.

Chieftainship declined, but clanship was more resilient, and lay
much nearer to men's hearts. The continuing sense of identity of
clan groups is shown by the slowness of highlanders to consider
marrying into lowland society, or even into clans with which they
had not had close dealings in the past.[39] Resentment of strangers,
not in any open form of discourtesy to them, but in passive resistance to their way of life, was one of the reasons for the failure of
many of the schemes for social or economic development of the
Highlands. We can see it in the eighteenth century in the failure of
the Dukes of Argyll to make their town of Inveraray, or their tenantry and servants, maintain cleanliness or economic efficiency.[40]

Bringing gardeners or innkeepers from the Lowlands to show how to do things did not prove as effective as the importation of English tenantry to reform lowland farming. Even more resistant to the 5th Duke of Argyll was his hostile tenantry from other clans in Tiree, until he modified his economic policy there.[41]

There was a genuine and persistent ethos among the lesser folk in the Highlands which kept them apart from the rest of Scotland, even while their chiefs accepted assimilation. We know that this was a period of literary creation. Gaelic culture, for many generations much more an aural matter than one of written word or visual art, was strong and creative, though attempts to bring schools to the Highlands made little contact with it. It should not surprise us to accept that in other ways too highlanders had their own norms and traditions. The emphasis on money as a motive remained alien for a long time. This is apparent in the most honourable aspect of the '45, the utter failure of a price of £30,000 on the head of the Prince to produce information about his movements. In some ways this slowness to accept financial motivation was still apparent in the Lowlands in the first half of the eighteenth century. Exasperation with it is a frequent note in Cockburn's *Letters to his Gardener*.

It is a common characteristic of undeveloped societies to be unable to set an acceptable price on services. Either too much, in the eyes of people more economically sophisticated, is asked, or much too little. 'One great reason for our people's living as they doe and not as they doe in England is the difficulty there is in getting things at all, and if to be gott they pay so dear for them, all sellers with us thinking of nothing but sharping a high price and sometimes for what is bad', wrote Cockburn.[42] We can find the same thing said by the guidebooks of the mid-nineteenth century for the Highlands. 'Numerous complaints have been received from tourists of the extortions practised in the Island of Skye', writes one. 'The charges made for guides, ponies and boats, are also complained of, and often justly...The evil, however, may be alleviated gradually by the wholesome influence which tourists exercise.'[43] (Travellers in the Highlands today may find it hard to accept as simply as this that they are doing the area a social service.) From another guide we have a complaint about the hard-fisted nature of the Scots in general modified by the remark 'in the isolated and sequestered districts of the far north the case is different, and the people are simple and unsophisticated. Twice in one day it was the good fortune of the writer to be refused taking payment for civilities rendered — first for a bowl of milk; second for being ferried across an arm of the sea...'[44] These comments should be regarded as different aspects of the same fact, the failure of highland society to accommodate to a set of money values.

This basic fact meant that the 'improvement' which was being pressed in the Highlands did not fit in with local values. The function of the improver was to make an estate increase its yield. He might see that yield in terms of rent, or he might see it in the total productivity, much of which went to a raised standard of living for the tenantry. In opposition to this was the peasant system of values in the Highlands where land was a means of supporting people and sustaining relationships between them. Since the basis of much of these relationships lay in the past, drastic change, even if obviously economically beneficial, was bound to be intolerable. The clash of the future lay there.

Another source of stress in the Highlands was sheer pressure of numbers. It became apparent as soon as law and order made it impossible to continue to maintain the population by forays on lowland resources. 'The land and number of inhabitants in Ranoch bear no proportion to one another, occasioned by their formerly living on the industry of their neighbours', wrote a forfeited estates factor in 1755.[45] The note was ominous. All parts of Scotland experienced a marked rise in population in the second half of the eighteenth century. In Highlands as well as in Lowlands, this seems to have been accompanied by an increase in resources, and in the transport arrangements that enabled them to be of use. Starvation, though still possible, seems to have become a less frequent visitor, rising again as a menace at the turn of the century. The trouble was that population growth continued and the standard of living was still appallingly low, housing squalid, food supplies marginal. More could not be got out of the land within the framework of the traditional way of life unless periodic starvation, also part of that way of life, was to be accepted too. By the 1790s, starvation was not acceptable to the governing classes throughout all Britain.

— Chapter 6 —

The Coming of Industrialization

'If it wasna' for the weavers whit wid they do?
They widna' hae claith made o' our woo',
They widna' hae a coat neither black nor blue
Gin it wasna' for the wark o' the weavers.'

The wark o' the weavers

IN the 1740s the most expensive possession of a skilled workman or a small farmer would be a mirror. In the 1780s it was a grandfather or eight-day clock. The change is significant. Obviously it shows the development of mechanical skills, and the increase in personal wealth. But the effect was more than comfort or richness. An awareness of time is one of the most important features of a labour force capable of industrialization. The Scottish child had for long known of time. His school day ran to long and regular hours, and so did his Sunday sermons. Now at home it was also regularly forced upon him. We have long accepted that there are characteristics that an economy must have before it can step forward into modern industrial production: wealth, markets, sources of power, financial services, skills. Only recently have we also come to see that there are social requirements too. Some of these come obviously from the economic requirements: enough inequality for wealth to be concentrated in a few hands; security of property from both civil disorder and arbitrary taxation; educational opportunities that encourage enterprise. Some are more subtle. For successful and smooth industrialization it is necessary that the owners of wealth be acquisitive as well as inventive, ready to take risks, and also to appreciate security. The labour force must be adaptable, docile and hardworking. The vast increase in population of the later eighteenth century put pressure on the work force and moulded it to fit the pattern of available jobs. A preoccupation with time is evidence of this moulding. It was a hard adjustment in a hard world, but one made easier by the priorities and practices of the Calvinist church.

To most of us the phrase 'the industrial revolution' conjures up a picture of factories. These are the embodiment of the new use of large-scale, powered production in certain manufacturing processes. In one sense, that of organized production of goods in one place, factories were not new. Besides the famous pin factory in Kirkcaldy, assumed to be that used by Adam Smith to illustrate the advantages of division of labour,[1] there were also weaving sheds in which men worked on individual looms; there were tanneries, potteries and other workshops which subdivided complicated processes into repetitive individual jobs. More significant of things to come was the large-scale ironworks at Carron, where water and steam power were harnessed. A scatter of other units — papermills, sugar houses and breweries — used large-scale methods and, sometimes, power sources. The linen industry had a proliferation of little mills, heckling and scutching mills in which water power reduced the monotonous labour of treating flax, and bulky machinery in bleachfields which 'manhandled' the finished cloth. What made the new factories 'new', the big spinning mills that started up in the late 1770s, was the scale of this mechanized industry, its use for processes that had hitherto been done in the home, and its need for a large market.

There still survives the industrial village of New Lanark, not with the original mill of the 1780s, for fire has accounted for most of the early mills, but with enough of the early layout to bring home the main features of this new world. A visitor to New Lanark can still wonder at the size of the mills. On the other side of the narrow cleft in the hills in which the complex lies stand the tall stone tenements of the labour force. This industrial colony is placed in open country, relying for its power on the rush of water over the falls of the stripling Clyde and cut off by a few miles of open moorland from the old county town from which it took its name. The main street is called Caithness Row: story has it that a shipload of families set out from the far north to emigrate to America, but were forced back by bad weather into the Clyde. By then destitute, they provided the colony's first workers, and gave the name of their homeland to the street. The most illuminating feature of the colony is the placing of the old mill office. It stands, and not by accident, in the one place from which you can see the entire village, and watch what goes on on every inch of open ground. In the new industrial world Big Brother was watching you.

A visit to New Lanark brings alive the new setting: the concentrated settlement of men and machines on a remote water-course, the heavy expenditure on mills and machinery, which meant that loss of mill-time was loss of money, the social discipline imposed on the worker on or off the job, the close-packed units in the one-roomed 'houses' of the tenement blocks which impressed on even the youngest the reality of corporate life. After early years spent in the houses of the mill, children would pass to the mill floor as workers, with their time off to be used in the mill school. The factory was a form of social education..

The immediate social impact of the rural spinning mill is described in the 1790s in the *Statistical Account of Scotland*. 'The numbers that are brought together ... the confinement, the breathing of an air loaded with the dust and downey particles of the cotton, and contaminated with the effluvia of rancid oil rising from the machinery, must prove hurtful, in a high degree, to the delicate and tender lungs of children . . . : Tempted by the wages, parents send their children to this employment at a very early age, when they have got little or no education; and the close confinement deprives them of the opportunity of acquiring more.'[2]

The number of people directly involved in this new way of life was at first not many. A mill might hold from 300 to 700 workers: there were 19 mills by 1787. In 1791 the mill at Blantyre employed 368, there were 660 in the two mills at Paisley with another 580 outworkers attached and spinning on jennies. It was estimated that in Glasgow in 1795 the total employment of the cotton industry was a little under 180,000, and that most of these people were outworkers of one kind or another. In the 1830s, though, mill work had become more common. There were 121 cotton mills then, employing directly 30,000 people. But more people still worked as handloom weavers.[3]

Until the steam engine became cheap and economical to run, the mill workers were mostly in remote places, where water power was available. There was, for instance, the great mill at Deanston, where elaborate use of the Teith ensured water all the year, there were mills on the upper Clyde, such as New Lanark, and on the edge of the Campsies. So long as industrialization was a rural phenomenon, its direct impact was limited. It was then possible, as it still is, for social evils to exist as much in small rural communities as in big urban ones. There has never been an urban monopoly of bad working conditions such as over-long hours and low pay, and petty oppressions and cruelty are more likely to continue undisturbed in the country than in town. But the social network of rural society, though strained, was not disrupted by a local mill. The mill workers made their own patterns of personal and economic links as had earlier home workers in industry. Middle and upper classes regarded industrialization with approval. It occupied vacant hours, increased family income, and did not change the basic hierarchy of the locality. Workers, farmers, schoolmaster, minister and land-owners still held their place and were known in their respective ranks. Occasionally someone, such as the minister quoted in the *Statistical Account*, had doubts about the physical and moral effects of the new activity on children, but all were agreed that idleness was bad for the young. As yet no one questioned that the new structure of industry was good for the community at large.

In the nineteenth century industrialization spread beyond the cotton-spinning mill. Weaving of cotton and linen became mechanized gradually, and in the late 1820s the iron industry began to expand on a new scale. But even when the new sector was small, it had ramifications beyond the valleys where the rural mills were perched. The well-known Kincardineshire song of pre-industrial industry, 'The Wark of the Weavers', proclaimed the security of these men:

> The weaving is a trade that never can fail
> As lang's we need a cloot to keep anither hale
> Sae let us aye be merry ower a bicker o' guid ale
> As we drink tae the health o' the weavers.

This song is a reminder of the great surge in creative force that accompanied the industrial changes, which produced scholars and poets among the workers. But it was wrong in its facts. Weaving as a trade did not survive the changes in a way that did any good to the weavers. The vast increase in demand, and the destruction of the apprenticeship system, brought people flooding into the trade to learn some sort of skill in a few weeks. Surplus population flowed into Glasgow, at first from nearby, later from Ireland and the Highlands, to overstock the trade. Weavers might work at home, but they were not independent craftsmen: they were the employees of the men who owned and rented out looms, and who assigned hanks of yarn. They worked for wages. Though the issue was not confined to Scotland, but involved the cotton weavers of Lancashire too, it was on the Clyde that the battle over the level of wages in the new, industrialized world was fought and lost by the workers in the years 1811-2.

In brief outline, this struggle was an attempt to move back to a world where prices and wages had some degree of public regulation. The English and Scottish weavers had appealed to Parliament for wage regulations. This was antipathetic to the spirit of the times and was turned down. A union of weavers was formed, and the Glasgow section took a table of wages to the judges of the Court of Session for approval. This they obtained, but the approval of the judges carried no weight with the manufacturers. When, in protest, the weavers went on strike they were arrested for illegal combination, and the Court of Justiciary (the criminal section of the Court of Session) brought in sentences of imprisonment.[4] When we seek for explanations of the hostility of working-class leaders in the later nineteenth and twentieth centuries to middle-class standards and culture, it is stories of this type of abuse of justice that provide it. The flowering of culture among the weavers of Paisley and Glasgow ended as they were forced into poverty and squalor, and the spread of the power loom took the process further. Handloom weavers became of use merely as auxiliary capacity in the industry. They became the misfits of industry, the men who could not or would not work under factory conditions at the factory's pace, but whose existence supplemented, to the profit of the factory owner, the mills in times of peak demand. They were the men who would work for a pittance rather than adjust.

Other ways of life changed with industrialization. Coal, already the main fuel of the country, became with the coming of steam, the main source of power too. Mines went deeper, which meant harder and more dangerous work for coal bearers. In the west the response was to increase the use of machinery for haulage, though even here some backward mines still used women and children for this crude work. In the east the industry was less efficient, and justified its primitive practices on the ground that it was genuinely difficult to use machinery on the slanting seams. The women and children were employed by the men miners. A child's 'bearing' would increase a father's wage from 4s. to 5s. a day, so the children had to work. We have some moving comments from them. Janet Cumming, age 11, who carried a half-load of a hundredweight from 250 fathoms down, was reported as having 'no liking for the work': 'father makes me like it'. There were stories of men rupturing themselves as they lifted these half-loads on to their children's backs.

The work was brutalizing and sometimes crippling. Hugh Miller describes the coarsening and distorting effect it had on women's faces. These were marked by a 'peculiar type of mouth, wide, open, thick-lipped, projecting equally above and below'; there was an exact resemblance to those in prints of 'savages in their lowest and most degraded state'.[5] Yet the miners were unwilling to see the work cease if this meant losing the extra pay, and employers readily acquiesced in the system. The government enquiry of 1842 commented that 'the hardships endured by the Young people... are such as to exclude the idea of any especial care of them on the part of the employer'.[6] When it was ended in 1844 the result was an increase in unemployment for the single women who had earned their living by bearing for an unmarried miner. These women were not able to earn their living in any other way. Some went on to poor relief, though in most parishes they were not considered eligible. At Carron we have it reported that some of the 100 women bearers, sacked because of the new regulations, had secretly returned to the mines. The ending of this type of employment involved many mine owners in expensive outlay, making the mines suitable for use by ponies or installing winding gear. This fact makes it unlikely that the use of human bearers had continued so long solely because it suited the male miners. There was never any suggestion, of course, of imposing on adult men work of the type that crippled their wives and children.

Industrialization speeded up economic life. Goods had to be moved about, towns and ports grew. Demand for food to feed the new concentrations of industrial workers put pressure on agriculture to improve in the north and west. The marketing system brought the effects of the new scale and price of production to every area, providing cheap goods, such as the products of the textile mills, and keeping up the price of food. The factory world set the pace and the prices of the rest of the country. Then this new sector cut loose from water power, and spread like an invasive plant into the towns. From about 1820 industry was as we have come to know it, urban. The existing towns expanded, and took on new specializations, or adapted old ones. Dundee, for instance, was a linen centre. Glasgow stood for cotton. Edinburgh continued to have a mixed collection of minor industries. But new towns were also created. The new iron industry in the west made Coatbridge and Motherwell. For good or ill the surplus population of the rural areas had to move to towns, and particularly it moved to the towns of the western part of the central valley. The concentration of people on the Clyde, which had begun in the late eighteenth century, was to make it one of the most densely settled areas in Britain.

What did this new, urban, form of industrialization do to the standard and quality of life of those who depended on it? The question has to be asked, even though no clear answer can be given. At least some of the facts that cloud the issue can be looked at. We have to remember that we are dealing with numerous groups and communities, and that a prosperous period for one may be a hard time for another. The flowering of the weavers has already been mentioned. Handspinning had, in the past, provided women with the means to keep alive, but it had done little more. Whenever the price of yarn rose the spinners were glad to do a little less of the monotonous work, and still they could earn the 2s. or 2s. 6d. a week that they lived on. By contrast, a young woman in a cotton mill in the 1820s, probably working hours no longer than in the past, could afford a little finery in her dress. Children could earn more than it cost to feed and clothe them. But at the same time, the old source of a little extra to the cottar's earnings, or those of the agricultural labourer, by his wife's spinning, had now gone.

Wages had risen in most occupations between 1770 and 1790, and even though prices had risen too, wages had risen more. Parish after parish in the *Statistical Account* tells of past wages, at 4d. or 6d. a day in 1760, 6d. or 7d. in the 1770s, and now at 10d. or 1s.: for instance Muirhouse in Angus reports that they are nearly four times what they were in 1760, Humbie (East Lothian) that they have gone up by a third in 20 years.[7] The rise was uneven, and had been greatest in the centre and west of the central valley. The process of industrialization was to increase the division that was already happening in standards of living between the prosperous south-west and centre and the rest of the country. One of the main reasons why agricultural wages went up in the richer areas was that they were pulled up by the higher level of urban wages. Farmers could not keep their labourers if they did not adjust to this.

Wages are only one part of the subject. There is the big question of the level of prices, and also the availability of things on which to spend wages. Certainly more material possessions were available, in greater quantity and better quality, than they had been in the past. It had become possible for labourers to aim at decency and cleanliness, to have a change of shirt or sheet at reasonably frequent intervals. Household goods of metal or pottery were more available. A family like that of Alexander Somerville, where the father worked as an agricultural labourer, could have, as a treasured possession, glass for a small window.[8] It became common to eat off earthenware. (This may not seem an improvement to those who haunt antique shops and value old pewter, but pewter, unless very regularly cleaned, is apt to give an unpleasant taste to food.) Housing was still cramped but usually more solidly built than in the past. The block of one-roomed houses that makes up the Livingstone memorial at Blantyre is a very vivid reminder of how limited this improvement was, and how much family discipline was required to live in seemliness in a Scottish tenement. But at least such a building was wind and water proof.

Even the new higher level of wages could be overtaken by the tremendous upswing of food prices that took place in the early nineteenth century. The growth of population had changed the country from a grain exporter to an importer, and the wars with France after 1793 brought price inflation as well as making import more difficult. There were several disastrous harvests, particularly those of 1799 and 1800, which sent vast numbers of destitute highlanders on to the roads, trundling their inadequate possessions in carts and hoping to ship overseas to Canada or America. In the Lowlands too these bad years compelled parishes to organize large-scale relief. Some bought grain to sell to the poor below cost and some even adopted a system like the English 'Speenhamland' one, of using parish relief to supplement low wages.[9] Even in years not as barren as these high prices had whittled away much of the gains of higher wages, and things were very tight for the labouring classes. 1810, 1813, 1816, 1818 were all difficult years, when families had little cash to spend after food was bought and many were hungry. It was because he had been born in the winter of 1810-1 that Alexander Somerville bore a lifelong grudge against parents who, he thought, had not been able to spare the few pence for registering his baptism.[10]

Even in easier years than these the enhanced wages still provided only hard living. In the country, whether in districts where wages rose in response to the draw of manufacturing, or in those where they remained relatively low, the total wage of an agricultural labourer, in money and kind, did not provide a family of a man, wife and three children with a diet that was adequate in basic elements. Even in the 1830s, when prices were more stable, wages, though nearer to this minimal adequacy than they had been in the eighteenth century, still meant malnutrition.[11] Urban wages were more varied, and some in the towns were doing well, but probably only the workers with a valued skill could hope to bring up their children without setting them to work or having their growth retarded by inadequate food. The deficiencies in diet were long-standing and enshrined in traditional patterns of food preparation and consumption that did not prevent families assigning money to other ends. Underfed children would still be sent, with their small fees, to school in the country. And of course in the town the new industry rewarded child labour at an early age.

Most of the workers in the new factories were juveniles, and a good many were children. The issue of the exploitation of child labour came to the fore with the ten hour movement of the 1830s. This was an attempt, initially by the workers of Lancashire and Yorkshire, led by the public-spirited mill owner, Richard Oastler, to have the working hours of children reduced in a way which would also have shortened the working day for adults. It resulted in the compromise Act of 1833 for cotton mills only, which forbade the employment of children under nine and restricted the hours of those under 13 years to eight in the factory and two at school. The particular interest of the campaign lies in the two contradictory reports produced on the relationship between factory work and ill health, and in the early workers' organizations that sustained the campaign.[12]

Neither of the two reports can be considered adequate as statistical evidence. That of 1832, which sets out to show that factory work produced crooked growth and deformity, displays no idea of the quantity of deformity to be expected in a 'normal' population. It conveys vividly the picture of individual mills with swarms of children (for each adult spinner had three children under him) working appalling hours and even then being expected to clean the machinery in the meal breaks. Children who fell asleep or flagged might be cuffed or strapped, and the combination of exhausted workers and unguarded machinery made for dreadful accidents. The hot, steamy atmosphere of the fine spinning which was Scotland's speciality was another unpleasant feature. Another was the primitive level of sanitary facilities, and the lack of opportunities even to use them. But it is also clear from this report that the 12-hour day attacked by Oastler belonged only to boom periods: in the recessions, which were now frequent, a ten-hour working day was much more the norm, though these hours did not include the extra work that children had to put in in the dinner hour: 'the children have barely time to peel their potatoes and eat them', was one comment.[13]

The picture given by the 1833 Royal Commission is equally unstatistical, for though the medical inspector carefully listed the cases of ill-health that he found in the mill population, the confining of the inquiry to the actual working population meant basing it on a self-selected sample, free of those already thrown on the scrap heap by ill-health. Though this inspector considered the postures in which work had often to be done 'unnatural', and thought that there was stress in keeping up with the pace of the machinery, the main disease which he associated with mill life was not deformity but tuberculosis. Here again we cannot make a clear statement on cause. 'Consumption' was the commonest cause of death in eighteenth-century bills of mortality,[14] but at the time 'consumption', though it included respiratory tuberculosis; also included other wasting diseases. We would expect the big, open rooms of the new mills to have been an excellent setting for the spread of tuberculosis, particularly since some of the workforce could be expected to have come un-immunized from rural areas free of the disease. Factory life probably enhanced the impact of respiratory tuberculosis, and by the mid-nineteenth century this was the biggest killer in the country. One observer points out that it was at its worst in Paisley, a centre of mill life.[15] But the medical inspector in 1833 also pointed out that income had a great deal to do with health, and that the workers in the cotton mills were among the more affluent of the working class. Stories of grisly accidents were confirmed in this report, but the evidence on sanitary conditions shows that this was often good. Certain physical defects, varicose veins, 'asthma' and other breathing difficulties, could certainly be attributed to mill life. It was rare for women to continue in factory work after marriage, so that the problem of combining work and pregnancy did not arise.

We are dealing here not only with the problem of evaluating unstatistical evidence, but of appreciating a radical change in the attitude of people to the proper activities of childhood. Most people today would accept that a 12-hour working day, even without this involving 13½ hours in the mill, or a ten-hour day which would involve 11½, are absolutely too much for a child, whether of six, nine, or 12 years old. Most people, however, at any period before 1900 would have been deeply shocked at the rules which we accept today which make it almost impossible to anyone under the age of 16 to contribute to family income. Given the normal parental habit of exploiting the labour of children, the existence of the large-scale campaign to get child labour curtailed and regulated is a *prima facie* case for accepting that there were obvious elements of overwork and impaired physique associated with the new factories, even if the medicine and the statistics of the day cannot convey to us clearly what these were. We should remember though that similar overwork existed outwith the factory system. Here is a brief note from the 1833 report on a handloom-weaving household in Bridgeton. 'Archibald Britton, age ten . . . Earns clear about 1s. per week; works as long as he can see. The father clears about 5s. per week. Working shop sunk below the level of the street; earthen floor; must be kept damp and close, otherwise the thread breaks. Food of this family porridge, potatoes and sour milk, when they can afford it. Very, very seldom meat.'[16] Archibald Britton would be unlikely to contract respiratory tuberculosis unless his parents were already infected, and drinking his milk sour would prevent contact with bovine tuberculosis. But long hours indoors in the damp would not encourage good health and he might have been doing better in diet in a mill such as Richards and Co.'s dry flax-spinning mill at Craig, near Montrose, where there was a daily dinner of potatoes, soup with meat in it, and sometimes fish.

The 1833 report also reminds us that even where the mill did not create illness, it brought home the issue of sick or hale in an extreme form. Here is the Muttree family in Dundee. Grace, aged 22, began spinning at 14 and rose to a wage of 6s. 6d., but she has been off work for 12 months with a short cough and a pain on the right side, and is thin and weak. Joan, aged 16, has not reached puberty, but is a spinner, in spite of pains in her knees and ankles and odd bruise marks that persist on her legs. Thomas, aged 14, is a tinsmith apprentice, clearly dying from scrofula (bovine tuberculosis), with two suppurating sores. Jessie, aged 19, has been a spinner for eight and a half years, and earns 6s. 7d. a week. Of late she too has suffered from swollen knees and distorted legs, and she has begun to sleep badly. 'A highly scrophulous family' is the inspector's comment.[16] Apart from the case of Grace, who is clearly suffering from respiratory tuberculosis, the diseases of the family are not such as would be directly caused by factory work, though the urbanization of industry may have been responsible for an increase in the likelihood of drinking milk infected with bovine tuberculosis. But one after another the girls of this family are finding themselves faced with a situation of no half measures. Either they work a full mill day or they cease to earn. Industrialization for the worker means, as did reorganized agriculture for the rural labourer, a system which does not carry the weaklings along with the strong.

Eventually the answer to the problems of the weak, or at least to some of them, was to lie in the organizations of workers. It is clear that for a time in the 1820s and 1830s the cotton spinners on Clydeside had achieved a high level of organization. There are reports about their control of entry into the occupation and of their high wages. There are also less attractive reports of the methods by which this control was maintained, of threats and violence. In January 1838 this came into the open in the trial of five of them for murder. At the trial it became clear that there was a long history of violence stemming from the spinners' union, which included three murders: arson, shooting and vitriol-throwing were organized activities, and the expenses of those committing them or getting away afterwards were entered in the union's accounts under code names. There were also payments for shipping inconvenient witnesses overseas. The union had been in existence since 1816 — a date when all unionism was illegal. Appropriately enough, its code word was Armageddon. The particular charge of murder could not be made to stick, even though the union had set about collecting evidence for alibis for the defenders before they were charged, and even though a defence witness who overdid total ignorance of various events had to be warned by a judge that there was such a thing as prevarication.[17]

It was to be market changes in the cotton industry, bringing stagnation to Glasgow and Paisley, which destroyed the powerful citadel of this group of workers, not the blacklegs (nobs they called them) against whom violence had been offered. It is depressing evidence of the limited sympathies of the 'system' of business and government interests that when the weavers had tried to protect their standard of living by appealing to the law, they had seen it disregarded, but when the spinners resorted to intimidation for a similar aim they were temporarily successful. *The Scotsman*, reporting the trial of 1838, commented in an indignant leader that illegal and violent practices against strikebreakers might have been justified if carried on by the handloom weavers, but that the spinners, earning between 20s. and 40s. a week, were among the highest paid of the country's workforce, and such action was therefore inde-fensible. Until the Combination Acts were repealed in the mid-1820s the only methods open to unions, which could not legally exist, were violent ones. It would be unreasonable to expect the aban-donment of these when unions were given the extremely limited legality of 1825, by which they were entitled to exist but not to act. In arson, assault and murder, society was reaping the evils which had been sown by repressive laws.

The spinners' case reminds us that an analysis of the standard of life for the workers must include more than consideration of goods and money wages. There is the whole question of security, and beyond that, status. A rural labourer had little status, but he had a fair prospect of employment from week to week. The town labourer had no such security. He himself could lose his job to another, or an economic depression could put works on to short time or close them altogether for months. The slumps of the business cycle appeared to be getting worse and closer together, and there were two severe slumps in the 1840s. Sir Robert Peel was to remark that he would never forget the destitution that he had seen in Paisley in 1841.[18] The mill-owner felt only a limited obligation to carry his workers in time of depression, and the Poor Law gave very little in the way of fall-back to the unemployed. Farm workers had greater security partly because they were hired by the year or half-year, but even so they could find themselves on the scrap heap through agricultural reorganization or continued depression. There was, for them as for the industrial worker, the basic problem of earning a living by manual strength which was bound to decline. The minister of Coldingham reported in 1844 that 'partly owing from long exposure to the vicissitudes of weather and partly from their diet not being of a generous nature, farm servants usually break down at a com-paratively early age. Their full working years may be said to be between 18 and 45'.[19] The treatment that such a man would receive in his premature old age would depend on the local climate of an inadequate Poor Law, and as yet there was no effective mechanism to improve on local inadequacies.

There is also a further sense in which the industrial worker was indubitably worse off than his agricultural grandfather, and that was in his expectation of life. The chances of death had always been higher in towns than in the country, and were to remain so until medical knowledge could explain the methods by which infectious diseases were transmitted, and local government organization control them. There was a pool of endemic infection in the big towns putting their populations at perpetual risk, and this was particularly serious in Scotland, a country which had for two centuries been adversely commented on for lack of sanitary facilities. The arrival of large populations with low standards of cleanliness would have strained a far higher level of provision than that accepted as normal in Glasgow, Edinburgh or Aberdeen. The risk of dysentery, and of 'fever', which covered both typhoid and typhus, increased sharply in the 1820s and 1830s. In the opening years of the nineteenth century the mortality figures of Glasgow, one of the few places for which reliable figures do exist, had improved sharply with the introduction of mass vaccination against smallpox, even though about a third of the children thus saved from death by this disease succumbed instead to the increased mortality from measles. Later a deterioration set in, and the death rate rose. By the 1830s Glasgow was notorious for its recurrent outbreaks of 'fever', and fever struck adults as well as children. The Infirmary had had fewer than 100 fever patients a year in the 1790s: it now had 2-3,000. If this fever was typhus, it was avoidable only by a high standard of personal cleanliness, since typhus is louseborne. If typhoid, it could not be avoided until the city was provided with a pure supply of drinking water and a sewage system. In either case, in total ignorance of the method of communication, the ordinary household could do nothing deliberately to reduce the risk. Families had to live in the squalor that came from packing population on a new scale into the high-built tenements, closed courts and wynds which made up the traditional Scottish urban landscape, and with no more in the way of public services than had sufficed for small rural settlements.[20]

We have many gruesome descriptions of urban squalor in Scotland in the 1830s and 1840s, and as they have a repetitive quality, one will suffice. In Greenock there was a dunghill in the street, described as containing 'a hundred cubic yards of impure filth, collected from all parts of the town. It is never removed; it is the stock-in-trade of a person who deals in dung.... The proprietor has an extensive privy attached to the concern. The effluvia all round about this place in summer is horrible. There is a land of houses adjoining, four stories in height, and in the summer each house swarms with flies . . .' and so on.[21]

Industrialization was at least partly caused by the population growth of the later eighteenth century, which fed it its labour and made its market. It was also the 'answer' to that population growth. Without the new resources of industry the population, growing at about 1.2% a year in the early nineteenth century, would have run into Malthusian disaster, famine or epidemic. The improved transport of this new world, the greater scale of marketing, the exports that paid for foreign grain, all prevented famine. But even though the industries of this period used a lot of labour, it is probable that the country had too much manpower for the available work. This kept wages low, and enabled employers to take long hours for granted. There was also a surplus of agricultural labour in the Lowlands, though the reformed agriculture was labour intensive. Men moved to the towns if they found no jobs in the country, but this movement was not yet fast enough to force up rural wages. Many areas had a good deal of winter unemployment: it is referred to by many of the witnesses to the *Royal Commission on the Scotch Poor Laws* in 1844 as part of the natural order of things.

On the whole, the lowland countryside achieved a rough balance between hands and work. The same could not be said of the Highlands, which were already commented on as overpopulated for their natural resources by many of the reports in the *Statistical Account* of the 1790s. The pattern of temporary migration, by which large bodies of highlanders would come south to work in the lowland harvest, was well established. In bad years, when the crops of the year before had failed to last into the summer, they would arrive in Edinburgh in large numbers before the corn was ripe, work for a pittance or be fed by charity. Yet if we take the population of the area that is geographically 'highland', it was only 115,000 in 1755: by 1801 it had become 153,000, by 1831, 201,000.[22] There had, of course, been some expansion of resources since 1755. The linen industry had become established in the fringe district of the Highlands, in Crieff, Comrie and Inverness. In Argyll there had been some success with woollen manufactures. Fishing had developed successfully on the east coast of Caithness, and many men travelled to it from the west for the summer season. The building of the 'parliamentary' roads after 1804 and the Caledonian Canal, financed partly by the central government to encourage highland development, had given work to many for a while and to some permanently. Higher cattle prices had, at least until the end of the war in 1814, brought in more money. We have a picture of the farming in the southern Highlands in the 1750s and 60s from the officials of the forfeited estates, which shows us how little of cattle and cattle produce had then been available for sale to lowland areas. By the end of the century trade was more active and prices better. But the change was not enough to lift the increasing population to prosperity. Many had left for Canada and America, and others had joined the army, but still the population of the Highlands was increasing faster than that of the rest of Scotland. Peasant landholdings were getting smaller and individual cattle stocks were falling.[23]

Two particular developments, though they brought money into the region, exacerbated the problem of overcrowding and small holdings. One was the encouragement of kelp manufacture, the burning of seaweed on the Atlantic shores for the sake of the alkali in its ash. This led to landowners, who received most of the profit of this activity, letting out minute crofts in return for labour on the shore. When the price of kelp fell in 1810 there had been established by then a concentration of people on coastal holdings too small to be viable. The other was the introduction of large-scale sheep farming to the inland straths. To make it possible to carry through the winter a sheep stock that would fully use the summer fertility of the hill pastures, the farming population had to be moved off the valley land. In the inland straths there had already been severe food shortages after bad harvests, which brought home the problems of bringing in extra food to inland areas. There was no likelihood of successful development of industries except where sea transport was available. So came the movement to shift the population to the coast, and encourage fishing or industries. However rational the basis of the change, as it came about it involved in many cases the compulsory movement of unwilling populations to a place and type of life they had no experience of and to a new system of hard and regular work. These forced migrations were the 'clearances', which still today play a large part in folk memory, and also in folk myth, in the Highlands. Since the 'industrial' development was not successful they led at best to the duplication of the poverty and destitution already experienced inland in more overcrowded conditions on the coast. At worst there was forced emigration to Canada or the United States. What the combination of economic rationalism and distant control by non-resident landownership could mean is shown in a callous instance referred to by Lord Cockburn which had led to violence and prosecution: 'it was said, or rather insinuated, that "arrangements" had been made . . . and, in particular, that a ship *was to have been* soon on the coast. But, in the meantime, the hereditary roofs were to be pulled down, and the mother and her children had only the shore to sleep on — fireless, foodless, hopeless.' Those who had, understandably, made a disturbance when they found their families put in this position were given short sentences with a rider from the jury that the action of the trustees of this estate, Solas in North Uist, was cruel, even if legal.[24]

No one who studies the relationship of chieftain to clansmen in the highland areas of the mainland in the late seventeenth or early eighteenth century can feel that it was free of exploitation. Chiefs compelled a naturally peaceable population to back up their own military ambitions, notably in the rebellions of 1715 and 1745, by threats of ruthless action against themselves, their houses and their cattle. But it is still lamentable that the chief-clansman relationship should, by the 1820s, have become a landowner-tenant relationship which allowed in some cases so slender a sense of responsibility on the part of the landowner. Even where, as on the vast Sutherland estate, the landowner did show a real, if inadequately informed, sense of responsibility, new policy might lead to severe clashes and a sense of wrong on the part of the peasantry. Part of the trouble came from the loss of leadership. The great landowners had seen the tacksmen, who provided local leadership and organization, as an unnecessary intermediate class: unnecessary to the new landowner, since he no longer needed them to organize the military strength of the clan, unnecessary to the tenants who could pay a lower rent if they did not have to support this local aristocracy. In some cases, for instance in Assynt, the tacksmen had cooperated in bringing in the new type of agriculture, and had proved useful to those above them and survived. In other areas they had been pushed out. Contact between landowner and tenant came now through factors, and sometimes these factors themselves wished to practise the new farming which would involve driving out the existing tenants. Where there were still tacksmen who looked at matters with the eyes of the older society, relationships might be good but the yield in rents low. If a landowner wished drastically to send up productivity he was unlikely to do it through such men.

Fundamentally the issue at stake in highland improvements, and particularly in those that involved clearances, was the function of the economic resource, land. It was an early example of the problem which has faced society very often in the twentieth century, whether resources should be regarded as exploitable in the interests of their 'owner' or of those who actually work and live by them. It can be compared, for instance, with the issue raised in the General Strike of 1926. Is the chief function of an economic resource, in that case coal mining, the maintenance of those who live by it in a way of life which they claim as a right, or is it production? The improving landowner expected his acres to produce crops and stock with the aid of the labour of whatever tenantry and labour force was necessary. That the 'profit' of these products would mostly come to his hands both he and his tenantry took for granted: that was, after all, what landownership was about. But if the function of farming was to enable a generation of highland crofters to lead the life of their forefathers, there would not be very much of this profit. And if, as food shortages increasingly made clear in the early years of the

nineteenth century, there were too many of them to be supported in
this style of life, there would soon be no profit at all.

The trouble was that the limited economic resources of these areas
and the assumptions of the rights of landed property meant that the
power of the landowner to reorganize his estates as he thought best
became a dictatorship over where people might live and how they
might work. At the same time convention expected more of a
highland landowner in social responsibility than of his lowland
associate. Most landowners responded to this responsibility, but
some did not. In either case, the opposition they encountered came
not from protest at this lack of responsibility but from refusal to
agree to drastic changes in the peasantry's way of life. The
Sutherland policy in the early nineteenth century was to compel
peasants to move to the coast, build themselves new houses and
undertake either industrial work in textiles, brewing or brickmaking,
or to combine small-scale farming with under-equipped fishing.
Even if this policy had emanated from people speaking the
language of the peasantry and living among them, even if the
material provision for the change had been adequate and ready in
time, it is likely that there would have been resistance.[25] The landowner here had already met violent opposition from part of the estate
over a matter not closely connected with the traditional way of life,
when he had attempted to install an unpopular minister in Assynt.[26]

Clearances, mitigated in some cases by unwillingness on the part
of landowners to use force, went on in parts of the Highlands until
well after mid-century. Even though many of the vivid stories told
about them can be shown to be untrue, the creation of these stories
of houses being burnt and people forced out shows that the method
and policy were felt to be ruthless. Some of the stories were true.
Unfortunately the economic policy of which clearance was the first
step was in the end a failure. The coastal industries other than
fishing did not thrive, and even the fishing was crippled by poverty.
A government inquiry in the 1840s found that a crofter could not
normally afford to buy the oars for his boat and the boat itself in a
single year.[27] Sheep farming ceased to pay, and eventually the
higher ground of the sheep farms was turned over to deer forest.
But until he actually left the land, whether to work in industry on
the Clyde or to go overseas, the highland peasant had a claim on his
landowner which kept him from the worst blasts of the cold
economic wind. If we compare the state of crofting families —
sustained, in squalid poverty, through the potato failure of 1846 by
their landowners — with the hardships of the equally squalid urban
poor as described in the early 1840s, we must appreciate that even
destitution can be privileged.

— Chapter 7 —

The Class Society

'There's a farmer up in Cairnie
Wha's kent frae far and wide,
Tae be the great Drumdelgie,
Upon sweet Deveron's side.
The farmer o' yon muckle toon,
He is baith hard and sair.
On the cauldest day that ever blast,
His servants get their share.'

Drumdelgie

I T is obvious that an industrialized society earns its living in different ways from an unindustrialized one. It is less obvious that this basic change affects matters not directly concerned with industry. The patterns of life within the workforce and the relations between workers and employers come to differ sharply in agriculture as well as in industry. Specialization, wages, the ownership of capital, all mark off men and families in their status. Movement from one group to another becomes difficult, especially across the divide between those who own and control the great wealth-making units of their world and those who are merely 'hands', units of labour. This is the dominant class division that nineteenth-century society created and adapted to. It made barriers not only between man and man, family and family, but between man and wife, parent and child.

In Hugh Miller's *My Schools and Schoolmasters*, the story of the self-education of a mason to the position of a world-famous scholar, there is an intelligent discussion of the way in which a man's craft dictates his bearing and conversation. Miller points out that tailors tend to pretentious fine manners, barbers to garrulous conformism, blacksmiths to independent taciturnity; shoemakers are careless, sensible and fond of observing 'St Monday', in other words starting the week with a holiday, carters, like all who live too much in the society of horses, are ignorant and unintellectual, and so on.[1] Using the same approach to the attitudes required for a man's work we can get some idea of the effects produced on people in changing from a working life in which, even if the load of work was heavy, there was still considerable freedom and choice in the pace and manner in which it was done, to a life where the pace was set by impersonal and relentless machinery, and the hours either by the factory hooter or by the man sent round to wake up workers in the morning. We should also remember the more immediate insecurity of employment, and hence of income. Before industrialization there could be a complete shutdown of work, such as that produced by the great frost of the winter 1739-40. There could be harvest failure, which would not only mean slow starvation for the peasantry but also quicker starvation for craftsmen, since with no money available for anything but food there would be no market for craft products. But these disasters usually came with warnings, threats of war, signs of bad weather, the visible failure of the corn in the ear to swell through lack of warmth or moisture. They had an impersonal inevitability. And they affected the whole of society. The new type of hardship sometimes came in the same foreseeable way; for instance the slumps of 1837 and 1843 could be seen coming. But the effect was still sharp. Earnings could drop from an adequate income to nothing within a week as unemployment struck. Unlike the peasant the industrial worker rarely possessed reserves of food in the house to carry the family for more than a short spell. At best there would be a sack or two of potatoes and one of oatmeal. There was also the risk of loss of income for the individual even in good times: accident, sickness, disablement, a reputation for unpunctuality or impertinence, might put a man off work any day. Losing a job would feel like a personal attack on his manhood, not a general disaster. In any case few men could take the pace of factory life after their late 30s. They would then depend, wholly or partly, on the earnings of their wives and children. This too could be seen as an affront to manhood.

It should not surprise therefore, to find working-class men creating a special social ethos with particular emphasis on the values of manhood. Strength was vital to a man's sense of himself, and rituals would be created to maintain it. One of these came from the belief among the miners of the eastern coalfields that washing the back could weaken it. As one of the mine inspectors noted, this resulted in permanently black backs.[2] (We don't have the comments of the men's wives on this aspect of personal cleanliness.) Longstanding habits in the distribution of a family's spending power, whether on food or on drink, would grow up to support this male emphasis. Certain elements of diet were regarded as peculiarly appropriate to the head of the household. Whisky, in particular, became enshrined in work rituals. 'Dram drinking', which had developed in the later eighteenth century, came to be linked with many aspects of life. It was felt that some forms of arduous labour put such an intolerable strain on men that 'ardent spirits' provided the only possible recuperation. This view was stated by Sheriff Alison in 1837 on behalf of the Glasgow cotton spinners.[3] The alehouse, or pub as it later became, was the main recreation centre available for all, and alcohol was almost the only commodity which could be bought everywhere in small enough quantities for immediate use. It was, after all, an age when 'shops' existed mainly for luxury goods, and food was obtained from weekly markets. Any impulse towards spending or indulgence was necessarily an impulse to drink or stand others drink. As whisky had replaced beer as the national form of alcohol, quantities of it could with relative ease be taken to places of work for celebration there. The amount of whisky downed seems very large indeed. We get a glimpse of it in 1823 when a new low level of duty took away much of the incentive for illicit distilling, in the Lowlands at least. In six months over three

million gallons were charged with the new duty.[4] This was
consumed by a population of well under three million (for in and
around the highland areas illicit distillation continued for reasons of
convenience), of whom over 40% were aged under 20, and many of
whom had incomes only just enough to live on. The average adult
of the Lowlands seems to have been putting away four or five
gallons of the hard stuff every year, which he could not rightly afford.
Hugh Miller commented that to him, in his youth, 'Use-
quehbae was simply happiness doled out by the gill'.[5] There was
clearly a lot of 'happiness' about.

The inescapably long hours of factory work cut men off from their
young children. A modern sociologist has drawn a picture of the
family as an entity going into the early spinning factories, with the
children working as piecers for their father and so under his control
all day.[6] This simply does not survive a critical look at the age
distribution of the factory population. A spinner in the 1830s needed
three piecers, or apprentices, and though the spinners restricted
apprenticeship, when they could, to relatives, it was still rare for a
man to have stayed in the factory long enough to have three of his
own children working for him. By 1837 the mixture of government
regulation and the nature of the work had got the small children out
of the mills. Most children at work in factories then were over 13, or
were prepared to pretend to be so that they could work the full day
of the spinner. A man would be out from his home for almost 13
hours in succession five days a week, and nine on Saturday. He
would extend this if he wanted a drink and some talk or company
with other men. We have a glimpse of an 'evening out' among cotton spinners in the evidence of those involved in the trial of 1838 —
a spell of putting the weight on Glasgow Green (a sport that called
for minimal equipment) and then a long pub crawl drinking whisky
in one after another of a series of low spirit houses, handing round
the single glass to each man in turn.[7] Such drinking places provided
one in ten of the city's habitations.

The new type of work in the new settings, the tensions as well as
the associations it set up, all altered the attitude of a man to his
family. Consciousness of lack of independence at work might be a
reason for insistence on mastery at home, and such an insistence
fitted in well with the legal presuppositions of society. A man might
see or hear his own small children only as the reason why he did
not get a good night's sleep when he needed it. Later, cut off from
communication by the din of machinery he might be conscious of
the failings of older children as piecers without any wider appreciation of their personalities. Adolescents might become rivals in

earning power, or even workers whose interests directly clashed with his, potential 'nobs' or blacklegs or, in the way of time, natural supplanters. Women who worked at the same trade were likely to undercut the price of his labour. His trade union, if he had one, would provide a sense of solidarity and friendship, but it was within a narrow group. The pressures of industrial work can explain many of the features of the social ethos of the later nineteenth century, the detachment of men from the affairs of their families, the confining of recreation on which money was to be spent to the male sex, the assumption that opinions and conversation on matters to do with work, politics or sport are unsuitable in the female. Below the respectable working-class family, where the man tried to hold a steady job and the household to live within its means, paying its way without borrowing, lay a vast section of the population which did not live respectably. These were people moving in and out of destitution and debt, who formed a floating semi-underworld of poverty and degradation. This was particularly marked in a city such as Edinburgh which did not maintain large high-wage industries. The searchlight of publicity lit it up for a while in 1828 in the Burke and Hare trial over the provision of corpses for dissection at Surgeon's Hall by the shortest and cheapest way available, murder. But there was a similar world in all the big towns. The respectable working man expected prudishness from his womenfolk because sexual promiscuity and prostitution were not only the inevitable life for women in this half-destitute world, but also the quickest way into it.

Sexual prudishness, and a desire to limit and control the activities of women, was one of the few areas where the more secure of the working class agreed fully with the middle class. In the middle class conventional standards of expenditure and a general ignorance of effective methods of birth control meant that men tended to marry late, when they could set up a handsome house and fill it with children. Prostitution was available to reduce the rigours of long abstention. The cool look that we have at this time of this social feature in Edinburgh in a book by the doctor of the local venereal disease hospital in 1840, shows how much middle-class demand, and in particular professional middle-class demand, was the mainstay of it.[8] The number of full-time prostitutes in Edinburgh was normally 800, but it fell to half this during the later summer when the General Assembly was over and the law and university terms finished. Middle-class families, well aware of the dangerous power of female sexuality, tried to rear girls ignorant of this power and of the seamy side of underworld life by drastic control of

AUTHENTIC

CONFESSIONS

OF

WILLIAM BURK,

Who was Executed at Edinburgh, on 28th January
1829, for Murder, emited before the Sheriff-
Substitute of Edinburgh, the Rev. Mr Reid,
Catholic Priest, and others, in the Jail, on 3d
and 22d January.

EDINBURGH:

Printed and Sold by R. Menzies, Lawumarket.

1829.

Price Twopence.

TITLE-PAGE OF "AUTHENTIC CONFESSIONS OF WILLIAM BURK."
(Edinburgh, 1829.)

communication. Literature had to be pure, and the lending libraries conspired with society to see that it was; sermons, if they mentioned the sins of the flesh had to do so in a code that could not easily be broken by the young and supposedly innocent, and of course, any direct questions should be evaded. 'When I asked what was False Sextus' "Deed of Shame", my father said, 'Oh, he was very rude to a lady', recalls Kathleen Haldane of her childhood in the 1870s; and, of a French novel she wished to read, 'when I eventually got the book some pages had been pasted over with brown paper'. 'This rationing of reading matter', she wrote in her old age, 'is one of the things which I have never been able to understand or, I am afraid, to forgive'.[9]

The 'protection' and 'control' which the middle class could exercise over women was, of course, much more complete than that of the working class. Working girls were bound to grow up with some knowledge of sex from the overcrowded conditions in which most families lived. The one-roomed 'house', the norm in Scotland whether in town or country, would be broken into compartments by box beds, but real privacy was not attainable in it, especially as it usually lacked a separate privy (ashpit was the usual euphemism). In any case such a girl needed knowledge for protection. She would have to mix with the outside world in going out to work and in marketing, even if the labour force at her job was not mixed. A middle-class girl could be brought up as a lady, and ladies were not supposed to walk about the streets unescorted or to enter the public rooms of an inn. Macaulay, writing to his mother about Edinburgh in 1828, said 'But you have not seen the town — and no lady ever sees a town. It is only by walking on foot through all sorts of crowded streets at all hours that a town can be really studied . . .'[10] An English visitor to Scotland, mid-century, referred to the 'stupid English custom which prevents the ladies of our country frequenting those places of public resort, of which gentlemen avail themselves', and called it the reason why 'they travel so little'.[11] ('English', in this as in many other writings of this period and later, from both sides of the Border, must be taken to mean 'British'.)

But in fact ladies did go about alone. They did so in the practice of good works, helping to run schools, thrift clubs, temperance societies. They gradually developed techniques and skills as social workers. If they were the wives of ministers they would go out to visit the sick. They might also go out to learn, to have music lessons or attend public lectures. Some of these activities may have sprung from frivolous aims, but it is worth remembering that the Edinburgh medical school was at least sufficiently liberal to allow some of the

pioneer women doctors to do part of their training there in the
1860s, and it was in Edinburgh that a hospital run by women for
women was founded in 1885. In the later nineteenth century ladies
could be found earning their living in activity outside the house,
usually in professional rather than industrial or commercial
activities, as teachers, artists, musicians. The male world was more
ready to let women take care of minds or bodies than of money.

In the long run this economic activity by women was to
undermine the assumptions in law and convention about female
disqualifications and female rightlessness, but this took a long time.
Before the assumptions on which law is based can be effectively
exposed as ridiculous the current of contemporary opinion has to
move a long way. There is little sign of rapid change in ideas before
the 1880s. The attitude of much of nineteenth-century society to the
idea that women might usefully be regarded as citizens with rights
and opinions had been shown in a minor exchange before a
parliamentary committee in 1847. The Free Church had come to
existence over the issue of the right of parishioners to vote on the
Call, that is to have a say in the choice of parochial minister. Yet
when its great leader, Dr Chalmers, was asked about whether
women could participate in this vote he replied 'I have always
looked upon this as a very paltry and distasteful question; I think
that it is revolting to the collective mind of the Free Church.'[12] A
hundred years before this date women can be seen participating in
Calls as 'heads of households' and nobody had described such activity
as 'distasteful'.[13]

Working-class women could not be kept from having a share in
the economic support of many households, though they could be
kept out of the organizations that working life threw up or the
recreations it made possible. Middle-class women could be kept in
the home in safety and comfort only by the expansion of the class of
domestic servants. Servants were recruited from the working class,
preferably from the rural working class, for it was widely believed
that rural society was more moral and less easily corrupted than
urban society. It was, at any rate, more imbued with habits of
deference. Though the hours expected of a servant were long, the
privacy offered negligible and the money wages low, the job gave
promise of physical safety, adequate food, clothing and warmth and
even the chance to save money. It was therefore attractive to many.
But it did not offer much in social mobility. Only if a girl could
become a cook, housekeeper or nurse could she hope to better
herself, and even these categories left her still definitely a member of
the working class. Members of the middle class liked to think that

they were part of a society in which a 'lad o'pairts' could rise to any position, but on the home front they wanted servants to know their place.

The theme of self help, of the ability of the able boy to make a career and rise in society, was a powerful element in middle-class thought. There are several well-known figures of the nineteenth century whose lives are used to illustrate it. Thomas Telford had been a shepherd's son in Eskdale: he had become a mason, and moved from that work to design bridges and canals, and become the greatest engineer of his day, first President of the Society of Civil Engineers. He was undoubtedly self-made, for his formal education had been simply that provided by the parish school in the 1770s. But his rise predates the industrial revolution: it was also purchased by giving up altogether the idea of family life. James Nasmyth had risen from his boyhood at the Edinburgh Royal High School just after the Napoleonic wars, when he spent his spare time casting brass in the fireplace of his Queen Street bedroom (one would like to have the housemaid's comments on the cleaning problems thus created), to apprenticeship in London with the great Maudslay, and finally to his own foundry on the Bridgewater Canal at Patricroft outside Manchester. But here the start was not from the working class. His family lay somewhere between artisan and professional, his father being a fairly successful portrait painter. Samuel Smiles himself, who rose through a medical career to high employment in the railway world, and who wrote both his *Self Help* and his own *Autobiography* to show how far the 'lad o' pairts' could travel, did not come from the working class either: his father was a paper-maker and general merchant. Adam Black, who came up through a bookseller's apprenticeship to run a successful publishing business, produce the *Encyclopaedia Britannica*, become Lord Provost of Edinburgh and a Member of Parliament, was nearer to working class in origin, but he had still started from the relatively privileged position of an education at the Royal High School in the 1780s.

The self-made man of the nineteenth century who had really known working-class life was Hugh Miller. He had experienced the rough life of a travelling mason, a craft in which, he said, it was rare to live beyond 45, which would involve putting up with 'housing suitable for a drove of pigs or a squad of masons'. The masons would settle in some comfortless outhouse, hay from the barn for their bedding and pot and pitcher as the only equipment, hanging their meal sack from the rafters to keep it from the rats, and go to work in all weathers out of doors.[14] With his chest already troubling him as a comparatively young man he had been ready to turn to

journalism and edit the contentious paper which became a spear-
head of the Free Church. But his career is not really evidence of
social mobility. Rather it points out that there were niches, places of
influence but of relatively low income, to which the self-made could
aspire. As in the eighteenth century a man of his origins could not
expect to get through to where power lay, the landowning class, so
in the nineteenth century the position of a captain of industry was
beyond his hopes. The social system allowed a dribble of able
people to move from the working class to provide specialized
services for the middle class, but this level of social mobility did not
mean a system of careers open to talents: rather one in which the
richer part of society collects a few valuable brains from the poorer.
The few people thus selected did not cause the social rift to close.

The opening of the great class rift in society cannot be dated
closely. It was not established in the early days of industrialization.
There is a delightful sentence in the *Statistical Account* for Rousay
and Eglishay, Orkney, in the 1790s, which states that there is 'no
difference in manners and habits between the cottagers and the
master... they all take social snuff together'.[15] That an incoming
minister should choose to make this comment suggests that things
were not so simple elsewhere in Scotland. Still, the main social gulf
in the 1790s was that between the small group who owned land and
the rest of society. At the trial of Muir and Palmer then for sedition
it seems that one of the reasons why Muir had been picked on as
victim was because he was one of the few advocates who came from
outside the landowning class, and his particular offence had been to
involve artisans in political discussion. It is also notable that Muir
himself felt it was degrading to have a servant called in to give
evidence against him, one of 'the meanest and the lowest', 'who
could hardly approach your presence even in their menial duties'[16].
Like many other 'democratic' Scots Muir did not extend these ideas
to the home front.

That a sharp cleavage between middle class and working class
there was in the 1830s is inescapable. It informs the outlook of the
New Statistical Account reports. It is shown in particular in comments
on the poor. The common theme of the *Statistical Account* reports
had been the inadequacy of poor law provision. Minister after
minister pointed out that the landowning class in rural parishes
usually escaped bearing a fair share of relief by being non-resident.
Only where the parish was assessed did non-residents necessarily
contribute, and otherwise poor relief came out of the church
collections. 'The poor are mainly supported by the poor' was the
theme. But the ministers of the 1830s had been trained in

universities under the intellectual influence of Thomas Chalmers, and Chalmers' immensely significant contribution to nineteenth-century thought was the welding together of religious and economic individualism, the doctrines of evangelicalism and political economy, with Malthusian fears of over-population. The ability to support oneself became a sign of religious soundness for all classes. In the middle class, bankruptcy became more of a disqualification for church eldership than was sexual misdemeanour. Working-class dependence on any sort of institutionalized help, other than the loving charity of neighbours and kindred, was a sign of degradation. Generosity in poor relief would encourage more dependence, and might even lead to encouraging imprudent marriage. This would increase the burden of dependence. Public aid to the poor would thus not only weaken the moral tone of the recipients, it would endanger society as a whole by the burden of new mouths to feed.

This attitude infused the questions put to the ministers for the *New Statistical Account* in the 1830s. They were asked whether there was or was not a deterioration in the 'natural reluctance' to claim relief, and not surprisingly most took up the lead and made replies such as this from Galashiels: 'the spirits of independence dies the moment that legal assessment comes to its aid'.[17] It is rare in this *Account* to find a minister who did not thus give his support to the landowning class in their determination to do all they could to avoid fulfilling their legal obligations by assessment, and when one does find such a minister, for instance Mr James Ingram of Fala and Soutra[18], he is, significantly, in a poor and obscure manse.

The more revealing statements of class rift, however, are to be found, as one would expect, in urban and industrial society. One document which could be expected to show it, and does, is a parliamentary inquiry into 'industrial combinations' (trade unions) in 1837-8. The language of class is conspicuous in the evidence from Glasgow. A master's comment on the unions is: 'there is a general belief that one trade supports another with funds; and there is a general feeling over the whole of the working classes in the trades that they are all bound; that they are all in one boat; and that if the spinners are put down, it will follow with the power-loom dressers.'[19] The spinners had been faced with sharp wage fluctuations, at one time a drop of 60 in six months, combined with the redundancy produced by the 'junction of wheels', and clung to their union. They said firmly that 'had it not been for the unions, our wages would have been reduced to nothing'.[20] One, when asked to agree that 'the masters had the best of it in the strike in 1837', remarked that 'they have always had the best of it in all disputes', but later added 'although we were beaten in a general strike, I am confident... that the dread of a general strike, by our employers, has prevented reductions in our wages': 'without the unions we would all be reduced to the same position that the hand-loom weavers are in just now.'[21] These statements appear true, and the conviction of their truth explains the bitterness and savagery shown to blacklegs. Sheriff Alison, called to give his opinion, said that there had not been a strike by a union in Glasgow 'in which intimidation did not begin the day after'. He held that 'reasonable aims', that is softening the blow of falling wages in depressions, could be achieved by a strike without violence: the violence came from an 'unreasonable' aim, that is an attempt to see that there was no such drop in wages at all.[22] Alison was sympathetic to working-class spirations, but even so the limited support that he could give to 'industrial action', his belief that workers should have the right to strike but not to picket or intimidate, shows how difficult it was for anyone on the other side of the class gulf to see how bad times could endanger the whole fabric of working-class life, and of course he accepted the doctrines of political economy which expected wages to take the main brunt of adjustment to bad times.

The middle-class attitude to the more disreputable or degraded of the working class was basically that such people formed a separate species. This is shown in remarks made by Members of Parliament in an inquiry into the workings of the New Poor Law in 1869. On the subject of the qualification for membership of local poor law boards a witness was asked 'Do you not think that the limit of £20 is rather too low, that it brings them too near to parties who would be coming on the roll?' There were references to pauperism as 'hereditary' and to a 'strictly pauper class'.[23]

Something approaching this sense of separateness can be found in the 1830s, when a government inquiry into the state of prisons produced the statement, 'Crime appears to be not only hereditary to a considerable extent, but also in some degree to belong to particular occupations'.[24] On this occasion it was not simply the dregs of society that elicited investigations. It was held that many occupations had criminal propensities: carters stole, colliers and fishermen went in for assault, and in general a lot of crime arose from 'combination'. Sheriff Alison, in a similar generality, which nevertheless looked more closely at the pressures on the individual, held that few working class girls could avoid being driven into prostitution, but at least in this case heredity was not called into play in the analysis.[25]

25 A late nineteenth-century scene at Poolewe, Wester Ross. By this
time crofters' houses were carefully thatched

26 The inside of an Islay cottage, 1772: the loom on the left makes it crowded and the hens on the rafters and the central hearth keep it dirty

27 Children playing in an Edinburgh street, early twentieth century

28 A farmer from Straiton farm, Liberton, under the Pentlands, has his ploughing and sowing recorded on his tombstone, 1751. Old-fashioned farming was a companionable task at which both sexes worked

29　The arduous tasks of Highland life were mostly done by women. Here, in Skye in 1772, they work at a handmill and also, with their bare feet, 'wauk' or felt a piece of cloth while singing

30　Sampling the product of an illicit still, nineteenth-century Kintyre

31 Camping out after eviction, North Uist, 1895. By this time crofters had security against all grounds for eviction save failure to pay rent

32 Inside a croft house near Loch Ewe, 1889. It is a cramped house and is damp because nets are drying indoors, but by now the crofter has a proper chimney, glass in the window and carefully made furniture

33 New Lanark, the famous factory village, *c.* 1825. Robert Owen insisted on education and physical recreation for the labour force. Here the mill children are learning quadrilles

34 a and b A Peebleshire tenant farmer and his wife, from an early eighteenth-century tombstone

35 Highland women gutting herring at Wick harbour, late nineteenth century. Gutting was dirty work which required a lot of stooping, so it was reserved for women

36 A modern copy of a 1786 illustration depicting work down the mine at Gilmerton colliery, Midlothian. Lothian mining was backward in machinery and relied on women and children climbing ladders with heavy loads of coal on their backs. The normal load for a woman was one-and-a-half hundredweight, and a young child would carry a quarter-load

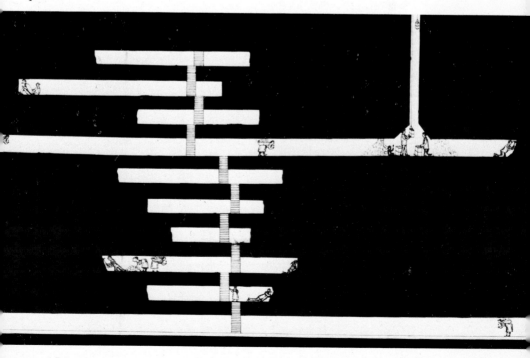

37 A near contemporary impression by a Swiss artist, David Morier, of the fighting at Culloden in 1746, the end of the last Jacobite rising

38 Scottish cities today have a reputation for violence: a recent razor attack in the main shopping street of Glasgow

It is not surprising that the working class, cut off from those above it not only by failures of sympathy and imagination, and by incompatibility of basic interest, but with the gulf accentuated by patronising generalizations, should formulate its own social and political institutions. Trade unionism is an obvious instance of something which must come from below to be effective, and it was not confined to the world of factories. An inspector of mines remarked in 1844 on the ubiquity of the system of the fixed 'darg', that is, the accepted day's work.[26] This, enforced by miners, stood at a level well below what a young active worker could achieve, and was the result of a real sense of social solidarity, the recognition that only by some such system could the older men be secure in their jobs. Employers and other members of the middle class would criticize this failure of workers to respond to the ethos of individual gain without appreciating their need for solidarity.

Trade unionism was not to have a place in the agricultural sector till late in the nineteenth century, though in parts of the country, notably the north east, workers on the bigger farms were creating mechanisms which enabled them to withstand pressures from their employers. The big farmer with several men working under him was as much a member of the middle class as a millowner. The practice of long hirings, for six months or a year, and the habit, in some areas, of housing the unmarried men in bothies, dormitory cottages singularly bereft of amenity, encouraged a special ethos and cohesion. Bothy life led to a resolute pursuit of pleasure in the small amount of free time left after the long farm day, and the pleasures were the obvious boisterous ones of drink, song and seduction. Song enshrines still much of this way of life, for the folk tradition of the north east, which may have still retained the ballad as a living art form into the later eighteenth century, more than 100 years after literacy was established,[27] had turned the old forms to a new content and created the bothy ballad. Instead of singing about lairds and ladies, magic, feud and war, men sang about drink and work and pleasuring the farmer's daughter. The ballad was no longer a form of oral poetry: it was written, and could be written to order. One of the most famous of these bothy ballads illustrates the way it could be used as a weapon against employers. The ballad *Drumdelgie* carries its sting in the tail:

> So fare ye well Drumdelgie,
> I bid you all adieu;
> I leave you as I found you
> A damned uncivil crew.

If the widespread singing of ribald songs about a farm was not enough to modify a farmer's behaviour, there was still one final weapon in the hands of his workers, the 'clean toun'. Bothy dwellers, married labourers, foreman and all, they would leave for new employment at the same hiring fair, and the farmer would have to start afresh with a new crew.[28]

The farm worker in the big farm did not need a trade union, and though his life remained hard and his income small, he lived in a real society, even though one which was constantly changing.[29] The urban worker had more need of social institutions to overcome his namelessness and loss of identity in the tall, uniform streets of the new industrial town. His trade unionism, when he could afford to support such a thing, was a weapon in a struggle for survival rather than a source of friendship and company. Unionism in Scotland was a long way away from the idealism of Robert Owen's conception. In fact Owen on his more visionary side, for all that he was based in Scotland, seems to have had little impact there. By its very generality his Grand National Consolidated Trades Union of 1834 was unattractive to men who had already a tightly organized union designed to make entry into their trade difficult and to maintain high levels of pay for a skilled minority. Owen's scheme for a communal village at Orbiston, which struggled from 1826-7, failed not only because it was launched in an economic recession. The basic flaw was that which has brought down most communes, unsuitable membership. Usually this takes the form that those who believe most sincerely in the beauties of communal living are to a high degree personally difficult to live with, whether from temperamental qualities or lack of cleanliness. At Orbiston dishonesty was one reason for failure: members embezzled supplies. Another was the imbalance of skills, which prevented it from being self-supporting.[30] After it failed Owenite millenarism seems to have left little trace on Scottish thought and practice.

It was otherwise with the major movement of the 1830s and 40s, Chartism. It is a historian's commonplace that Chartism, ostensibly a working-class movement for simple parliamentary democracy of the one-man-one-vote type, was powered by economic distress and tended to be weak in boom periods. It is also a commonplace that the movement contained the advocates of moral force only as well as of physical force or violence. But these two sections were not really distinct from each other. There were many Chartists who were uncertain in their attitude to law and order. They would refrain from violence if it looked as if 'moral force' alone would bring results. Scottish Chartism tended to belong in this grey area. There was a lot of talk about 'conditional obedience' to law and order. It was not a good time to be open in the advocacy of violence, for Chartism started up in Scotland at the end of 1837 when the trial of the cotton spinners was coming up. But in any case Scottish Chartism was not an exclusively working-class movement, and its political philosophy did not argue in class terms. There were elements of an older radicalism, the atheistical movement of the 1790s for which Paine's *Rights of Man* had replaced the Bible.

There was also an attempt to give Chartism a religious element, to found 'Chartist Places of Worship' and hold 'Lord's day' services in them. This aspect failed through refusal of the churches to co-operate, though one minister went so far as to bring out a book of *Chartist and Military Sermons*. The general failure of Chartism is usually attributed to the depression of 1847, but in Scotland most of the steam had gone out of it by 1843. High unemployment in the cotton industry wrecked it in the west, and, significantly, the Chartist newspapers were already failing in 1841.[31]

But Chartism was not totally lost after 1848. The residue of the movement moved on to join middle-class radicals in pressing for parliamentary reform. More important though to working-class life was the memory of a period in which a common aim, and for the most part common methods of action, had held together large bodies of working men. The characteristic emphasis of later working-class movements on democratic voting, parliamentary methods within and without the House of Commons, the influence of the news-paper leader and speech rather than pieces of paving stone as instruments of political expression, all stem from this time. It was impossible to maintain an organized movement for any length of time on the spare cash of the working class, given the incomes of the 1840s, but Chartism showed that working men had the social and intellectual ability, if not the means, to keep such a thing going.

The attempt to link Chartism with organized religion reminds us that religion had a strong hold on all classes. A church congregation would form one of the recognizable and understandable units to newcomers in the great towns. Working men were not often part of the inner circle of government of these churches, the kirk sessions, but all took part in and appreciated the arguments of the great storm that shook the church in the 1830s and 40s and which resulted in the Disruption of 1843.

This storm can only be understood by an appreciation of the special content of evangelical thought and expression that had continued in Scotland throughout the eighteenth century, partly contained within the church. It was a deeply moving and personal form of Calvinist dogma, best understood from the sermons of Ebenezer Erskine, which explore relentlessly, yet with ever fresh and renewed impact, the meaning of election and salvation. Erskine's sermons are probably the finest religious literature that Scottish protestantism has generated. He and his followers had moved into separation in the 1730s, and there had been later offshoots and divisions as well, but a large element within the ministry continued to hold that its function was to present the great dogmas of election and assurance, of reprobation and damnation, to its flocks. To preach the application of religion to everyday actions was to preach 'coldly' a 'mere Morality' (in the language of evangelicalism). The section of the ministry that stressed morality was that of the moderates, who also held by accommodation with the secular sources of power, on the grounds that the church in the world had to recognize the authority of worldly government. The combination of opinions gave to the popular mind an association between evangelicalism and non-cooperation with government. On to this continuing populist strain of opinion came the evangelical revival of the late eighteenth century. This revival was Calvinist, but its emphasis was less on dogma and more on its social expression, on good work and righteous causes as the fruits of conversion.

Evangelicalism carried with it, as Calvinism had often in the past, its own particular streak of worldliness. It was not the role of Christians to refuse the worldly goods that the economic system brought to them, or to endeavour to change the basis of society. The Christian duty was to purify one's own heart and enlighten others. Such worldliness might have been no more than a background feature, but the political fright of the 1790s, when atheism, French power and radicalism at home were all thought to endanger society, pushed organized religion, whether moderate or evangelical, into unquestioning support of the existing political, economic and social order. Moderatism went over most completely to conservative subservience: since one of its leading themes was that the church should co-operate with the state, it became easy for it to become completely servile. The evangelical wing accepted the social system uncritically but its long resistance to one particular manifestation of state power, patronage, made it less servile politically.

Patronage, the right of lay patrons to nominate a qualified minister to a parish, had been reimposed on the church in the early eighteenth century. By the end of the century the church had stopped formally protesting about it, but resentment remained. While there was no great difference in religious thought within the church, or while such differences as existed were as evenly spread through the landowning patrons as through the more vocal parts of the church as a whole, lay or ecclesiastical, it worked smoothly enough. It could also work smoothly if patrons busied themselves effectively in parish matters, functioning actively as elders for instance. But by the early nineteenth century many landowners did not reside regularly in the parishes where they held estates. They might pass the winter in Edinburgh, seeing to the education of their children, going to parties or adding professional earnings at the law to their landed income. They might own land in several parishes. In any case in a time of political stress and adjustment, when radical thought was considered a threat to property, the upper classes tended to see their interests as lying in the total preservation of all species of property, and by the law of the land patronage was a form of property.

The church was trying to adjust to a new world. It was a world with new kinds of social stress, and with new concentrations of people. The church needed to create new parishes, and the clamp of patronage made this difficult. Evangelicals within the established church could not help envying the freer hand of the dissenting evangelicals in adjustment to the new distribution of population. They could see that the main problem of a dissenting church, the need to raise funds directly from the flock to support both buildings and ministry, could by active organization be made a further source of strength. They could also see how the right of a congregation to choose its own minister bound that minister and congregation close together. In an effort to hold its own with dissent the General Assembly in the early 1830s altered the rules about the status of churches and patrons in a series of 'Acts': among these the important ones were the 'Veto Act', which gave to 'male heads of households' of the parish the right to refuse unpopular ministers, and the 'Chapel Act', which enabled new parishes to have almost as much autonomy as old parishes. Both these measures not only aimed at reducing the hold of patrons on the church, but also weakened the share of the more conservative element in the ministry within the courts of the church.

The 1830s was not a period when the rights of property could be destroyed without resistance. These were the days when a highland landowner felt entitled to evict his tenants and a factory owner held power not only of dismissal but of drastic reduction of wages. Parliament and lawyers saw the church's 'Acts' as attacks on existing law, and the lay courts reasserted the existing law of patronage in a crude form. For ten years test cases divided the church and nation into two bodies. The emphasis of what lawyers called 'the wild party' in the church on evangelicalism and popular choice brought a great deal of popular support to its side. Finally, in May 1843, when Parliament refused the claim of the church to what would have amounted to the right to define the legal content of 'establishment' and patronage, the church split. Established church and Free Church drew their congregations apart. The Free Church set out to create in itself the mirror image of the established church: buildings, ministers, schools and societies all had to be at least as well provided as in the establishment. This process gave it great material preoccupations. It was now to experience that dissent might mean the exchange of state control for control by the moneyed section of the people. It is typical of the imitative and conventional opinions within the Free Church that it insisted on building stone churches (brick in Scotland was material suitable only for outhouses until the twentieth century) and stone manses on land held on long tenure and preferably next door to the established church. Short leases, adapted buildings, flimsy structures would not do. If denied feus, it would ape the stories of the covenanting period and meet in the open, while loudly protesting that this was very bad for the health of the ministers. The health of the congregations did not figure in these protests.[32]

Since the justification of the Free Church lay in popular support it had to encourage hostility to the established church. At the level of ministers and elders, the government of the church, this hostility was real enough, for there had been confident expectations that the whole of the church would have stood together in resistance in 1843. Those who had decided to stay in the established church were backsliders from the cause. Free Church journals denounced the Church of Scotland as lacking the features of a true church. The populace used cruder phrasing. As people went to the established church on Sunday they might hear the urchins of the other persuasion singing

> The walls are thick,
> The folk are thin.
> The Lord is ga'en oot,
> The Deil's come in.[33]

The raising of the financial basis of the new church is a more admirable picture than this vendetta, a tale of business skill and courageous foresight. The foresight, once understood, in fact reduces the element of courage in it, for the plans and funds were already there or promised in May 1843. The ministers who marched in the Disruption procession down the Mound and up Hanover

Street to hold their own Assembly were embarking on a life which would involve new relationships with their flocks, a new structure of organization but not an immediate risk of penury. In a very real sense the people who paid for this splendid display of religious independence were the poor. Voluntary contributions had for many months been channelled away from the normal system which maintained poor relief,[34] and continued to be after the Disruption. The Free Church did not formally refuse to support its own poor, but its dependence on its capacity to screw contributions out of the congregations meant that money simply was not available for the older purposes of parish funds. It also meant that churches could not survive in the cities unless they had at least a part of their congregation in the richer areas, and most of their seats rented out. This was another motive for the Free Church habit of placing its churches in good and central places, preferably up against the established church. The main advantage, after all, to a church in being established is that it rests on battles that have been fought in past centuries over who is to pay how for its support. The Free Church had to fight this sort of battle year by year and month by month. More and more it found itself tied to the middle class. It made gestures in the direction of poor relief, but most of the charitable funds of its adherents went on sustaining the structure, and the main burden was left to the reduced membership of the established church. Since the Disruption occurred in a depression year, this brought forward urgently the need to reorganize the Poor Law, now patently incapable of functioning.

A limited amount of reform was therefore doled out to the Poor Law in an Act of 1845. This Act accepted what had become a basic feature of the Scottish system, that 'mere destitution', usually resulting from unemployment, was not a sufficient qualification for relief, in spite of the widespread evidence that this was an anachronism in an industrialized society. But it set up a structure of central control which gradually forced parishes to make adequate provision for those who were qualified for relief, the old and infirm, orphans, the blind and sick, widows with young children, etc. A person denied relief could appeal to the sheriff court: legal responsibility for the denial rested on the paid inspector of the parish. Every parish had to have such an inspector, full or part-time, and once appointed he could not be sacked without the approval of the central board. This mechanism put steady pressure on parishes to discharge their responsibility more generously, and the result of this was to bring many to raising funds by assessment. Within a few years half Scotland's parishes were assessed. Before this new system, the only part of Scotland where relief had been given in adequate amounts was the Borders. In the north-east parishes had pretended that 6*d*. a week, or even in some cases a mere 10s. a year with licence to beg, was enough for a pauper to live on. (For an appreciation of the value of these sums it is worth remembering that 2¾*d*. a day was the minimal cost of feeding a prisoner in gaol.)[35] These parishes had now either to raise much greater collections or set up a system of assessment.

Before 1845 resistance to the principle of assessment had been sustained by the arguments and work of the most influential minister of the day, Thomas Chalmers. Chalmers held, to a high degree, a sentimental nostalgia for rural life which was widespread in the church. He looked to the countryside, and particularly the countryside of an earlier generation, as the basis of moral strength, and, reared in northern Scotland, his first charge had been the country parish of Kilmeny, Fife. (Kilmeny was a parish which excelled in meanness of provision for the poor.) Later Chalmers was to try to reduce a large urban parish in Glasgow to the same low level of mutual support. He was to claim that this parish, St. John's, created for the purpose of the social experiment, and containing 10,000 inhabitants, was able by organization and systematic pressure to get rid of assessment. The poor who asked for aid were visited by deacons of the church, and their cases investigated. In most cases the burden of aid could be shifted from the parish, where it statutorily rested, to relatives or neighbours. Chalmers claimed a great success for the principal of individual self-support and voluntary contribution. The claim was intellectually dishonest. His parishioners had been a floating group who could and did easily move into neighbouring parishes if denied support in St. John's, and neither he nor his deacons put enough time into the work of investigation to make it other than very summary.[36] But the propaganda that his experiment allowed and encouraged against a more adequate concept of the duty of mutual self-support was one of the reasons why the reform of 1845 was limited in its concept and cautious in its mechanism.

Irrespective of the claim that it was a part of Christian morality not to sustain a larger section of the poor than was absolutely inescapable, there was a pressure by landowners to return to the older and more ineffective system after 1845. The inadequacies of the new law were supplied, as before in economic crises, by voluntary subscriptions. Such voluntary aid, with government organization, and large-scale financial support by the local land-owners, carried the Highlands through the potato famine of

1846-7.[37] Subscriptions were raised in the big towns in times of depression to sustain the unemployed, otherwise excluded from relief. We have a sardonic comment on the motivation of subscribers in evidence given before a select parliamentary committee set up in 1869 by those who wished to get back to the situation as it was before 1845. 'In 1848 . . . this liberality, which ought to show itself at the proper time, did not . . .; the result of that was, that the dissatisfaction broke out into open violence, various shops were broken into, and the loose class of the city threw themselves into the mélee . . . in one evening, damage to the extent of upwards of £9,000 was done; and then of course we were obliged to send the hat round immediately . . . £9,000 of police repairs would have relieved them for a very long period.'[38] Another witness in the same inquiry remarked that 'the magistrates of Glasgow, or any other great town . . . always wait until, if they did not come forward, it would almost end in actual rioting'.[39]

In practice the reformed Scottish Poor Law was a more humane institution than might have been expected from its limited remit. Those who worked in it were all the time handling cases of real, often acute, need. They rapidly removed themselves from the view, expressed by a member of the 1869 committee, that the function of a poor law was to get rid of claims for relief, and developed a structure that did its best to make life comfortable for those accepted as entitled to aid. Houses were built to protect the old, orphaned children were boarded out in the country, and of course also sent to school, dispensaries and hospitals set up. Free from the burden of supporting those whom many wished to deter or discipline, the unemployed (in other words by ignoring the most difficult area of the problem of poverty which might arise equally from fecklessness or from the malfunctioning of the economy), the Scottish Poor Law was able to offer a humane system to the rest of the poor. Even so the parochial boards had to face some disciplinary problems. They met these with the technique in tricky cases of offering relief only if the applicant would enter a poorhouse. This choice, resembling the English 'workhouse test' was not regarded as a deterrent but as a means of distinguishing genuine need. Still, it was disciplinary in some cases. In 1870 the inspector of New Deer remarked about unmarried mothers, that 'the poor house test is very beneficial', a remark which has a distinct flavour of 'spare the rod and spoil the child'. Also, disabled paupers were not so disabled that they could not indulge in tiresome practices. One reason why Edinburgh actually built a big poorhouse in what was then distant country was the annoying practice of paupers resident in the old poorhouse in

Bristo Street of climbing out of the poorhouse for a drinking bout financed by the sale of the clothes provided by the board. When sobered up they would then have rightful claims for readmission, as well as for new clothes. This became less easy in the rural seclusion of Glenlockart.[40]

The change in the Poor Law was only one of the changes made as society grappled with the social problems of industrialization. Already an attempt had been made in the 1830s to set up a system of middle-class democracy to govern the towns, which would be relatively clear of corruption and able to provide the minimal services, street cleaning and market control for instance, which went under the head of 'police'. The existing burgh councils, described in far too rosy terms in Galt's *The Provost*, were put on a wider franchise and their powers of corruption somewhat limited, and for more effective government citizens could apply to have separate police burghs run by elected councillors. The clumsy set-up of parallel institutions was one way of combining historic continuity and minimal standards in essential services.[41]

Other institutions also had to be reformed to bring Scotland into the modern world. Increased medical knowledge and the developments of modern life in transport and machinery made it sensible and humane to arrange for some better regulated care of lunatics than had been achieved either by infirmaries or by the Poor Law. Scotland's gaols had been under criticism for some time. Some of them were squalid holes; Forres for instance. Some were shockingly insanitary. At Brechin there was no privacy at all for either sex, even in sanitary matters. In Aberdeen a convicted coiner had set up shop again in one of the day rooms of the prison. But the main complaint about imprisonment in Scotland was that it involved merely a relaxed and convivial stay with plenty of whisky and visitors, and that in most cases the stay was strictly voluntary. At Brechin the entire gaol population was said in 1836 to have run away three years before.[42] That this abscondment did not happen oftener was probably because of the boisterous whisky parties allowed. Lord Cockburn refers to a failure of security over a prisoner who was thought too powerful for the gaol at Alloa. 'They hired a chaise and sent officers with him to the jail at Kinross, where he was lodged. But before the horses were fed for their return, he broke out, and wishing to be with his friends a little before finally decamping, he waited till the officers set off, and then returned to Alloa, without their knowing it, *on the back of the chaise* that had brought him to Kinross.'[43] Reform, which came eventually, involved the building of one interesting prison, that at Jedburgh, which has now become a museum. Here the aim was to provide a regulated and improving atmosphere and a level of physical comfort far above that of the ordinary labourer. It was a true attempt at reforming the criminal by environmental means.

For the most part the reform of prisoners in Scotland meant imposing the repressive 'separate' system, devised in America, which made long sentences fearful and disabling. The prisoner was supposed never to see or speak to any human being except the officials of the prison. A loaded report by a government commission urged the merits of this system in 1840. The commission had some difficulty in answering objectors who held that there was no distinction between this system and the solitary confinement which was used as a punishment for prison troublemakers. The main distinction, said the commission, was in purpose. The aim of this separation was reformatory, of the other, punitive. But it was also stressed, in a manner that implied that the objectors were right, that a distinction lay in the higher level of comfort provided in food, lighting and exercise.[44] It was in fact penal solitude, under conditions used by modern 'factory farmers' for calves. The system was gradually imposed on the various gaols of Scotland, and in the process these places had to be made efficient, well manned, clean and orderly. The system ended most forms of contact between the outside world and the prisoner, and so respectable society was able to live in ignorance of this section of the unrespectable and the treatment meted out to it.

At the same time modern police forces were being founded, which made possible some control over the scale and location of crime. Policemen were also of general importance in the multifarious business of a complex society. They would, for instance, control drunks, even though they could not prevent drunkenness, in the interests of society as well as of the drunkard, and often with real kindliness. Some forces invested in special wheelbarrows for taking drunkards home.[45] They would regulate traffic of all kinds. Their watchful presence encouraged the criminal and the prostitute to confine their activities to parts of towns which were not, on the whole, the residential areas of the better-off.

Among all the important institutional reorganizations of the nineteenth century, of which only a sample are mentioned here, the laggard was education. Scotland's parish school system continued to function in the rural areas of the Lowlands, and a collection of cultural and religious societies created a miscellaneous network of small schools which had some impact, but not much, on the Highlands, but in the big urban centres there was both a lack of schools and an unwillingness of families to use those that did exist. A single-teacher parish school could not hope to cope with the needs of a parish of ten or fifteen thousand people: if an assistant teacher was provided the professional standard of the principal teacher might be so low that he took it as an opportunity for idleness. The lack of adequate schooling for the bulk of the poorer section of the population had already been conspicuous even before children could make a useful contribution to family income in the new factories. Factory legislation and technical changes gradually got the younger children out of the cotton mills, but there were many other industrial openings for nine or ten-year-olds, the tobacco and 'gutta percha' (rubber) works in Glasgow for instance, uncontrolled by legislation. There grew up a proliferation of small schools, one-roomed basements providing child-minding and a visual acquaintance with the alphabet, and little more except opportunity for the exchange of various infections. These were 'adventure schools' from which partially educated teachers, unlikely to find a living by any other occupation, kept body and soul together.

The remains of the professionalism of the old Scottish approach to education achieved two major advances in the first half of the nineteenth century. One was the creation of a recognized status of teacher: qualification and career were to some degree defined when the Educational Institute of Scotland was set up in 1847, but this rested on a great deal of earlier work in the establishment of 'normal schools' and colleges run by the churches. The formalization of status may, in the long run, have been responsible for a certain defensive determination to run education by categories, by fixed subjects and fixed qualifications to teach such subjects, which has in the long run imposed rigidities on Scottish education, but it prevented schooling being merely a means of social control of the lower orders by their betters. The other advance was a start, a hesitant one, in the work of adapting the Scottish universities to the task of producing the trained manpower of a modern society.

The universities had for long been training ministers, lawyers and doctors, but their success, such as it was, in these areas meant that the faculties concerned with such specific careers were preventing the rest of the universities from providing effectively the more general education needed by schoolteachers, businessmen or servants of the state machine. Government plans for reorganisation in the 1830s failed, but the universities themselves began to change. The scale of accepted priorities is shown by the fact that the most successfully and rapidly adapted sector was the medical. The outside world needed doctors urgently, and this was the way to get them.

If we look round the Scotland of the 1850s and 1860s we can see a recognition, often a real fear, of problems, by the middle class. Slowly institutions were being adapted to cope with them, political institutions, local institutions, voluntary societies. The tasks were not easy, and not all decisions made were wise. While the working class created the defensive features that maintained status and standards for some at least, the middle class was moulding a new society.

— *Chapter 8* —

Images of
Modern Scotland

'Oh ye canna fling a piece frae a twenty storey flat,
Seven hundred weans'll testify tae that,
If its butter, cheese or jelly, if the bread be plain or pan,
The odds against it reaching us are ninety nine tae ane.'

Glasgow song of the 1960s

S COTLAND is and has been a country of diversity and con-
tradiction. Some of these features have been the product of her
varied geography. For a country small in terms of population she
spans a great variety in terrain, from the prosperous farmlands of
the south-east, and the industrial concentration on the great estuary
of the Clyde, to the leaner farming of the north-east and north and
the old bare rocks and scattered lochans of the north-west and the
outer islands. She has also a mixture of peoples not fully blended;
the Norse in the far north, still clutching their tenuous traditions of
links with a neglectful Scandinavia, the Gaelic enclave on the north-
west separated by a different first language from the rest of Scotland
but separated also by religious and historical rifts from fellow Gaels
in Ireland, and even in the English-speaking heartland the vast
differences in speech, personality and ambitions between the folk of
the east coast and those by the Clyde. There is also the longstanding
sense of kinship with people overseas, people whose ancestors left
Scotland in the nineteenth century to better themselves but who are
sentimentally labelled 'exiles'. Sentiment hangs on less affec-
tionately to those who from similar motives went to England in the
nineteenth and twentieth centuries.

The muddle over 'exiles' reflects emotional confusion. If carried
out logically the concept could cut off from the body of Scotland all
those who came to the country, from Ireland in the nineteenth
century or from England in the twentieth, and, more pre-
posterously, their Scottish-born descendants. The incomers must be
considered as much a part of present Scotland as those whose
ancestral intrusion lay some centuries earlier.

Given the variety of peoples and experience it is impossible in a
short space to convey the full variety of life in the last century. It
seems best to approach modern Scotland through the contrasting
images of the country that are held by Scots themselves, by people
of Scottish ancestry and by outsiders who have seen something of
the country. These images always contain some truth. The fault of
holding to them is that it is dangerously easy to think that any one
image encapsulates the life of this nation. By illustrating the last
century in Scotland through several such different images I hope to
avoid this pitfall.

Scotland the Religious

First of all in history and at least notionally in the priorities of many
Scots today, must come the image of Scotland the religious. By

religious many mean Calvinist and presbyterian. Such a definition ignores the considerable element of Roman Catholicism, both in the form of the old Catholic enclaves, for instance some Western Isles, and the Catholics of Irish provenance, the result of the nineteenth-century immigration. The latter is the more conspicuous section, not only numerically but because it has supplied the structure of the church. The Catholic priesthood of the late nineteenth century was recruited in Ireland: service in the poorer areas of lowland Scotland, where Irish immigrants filled the lower paid jobs, was an alternative to missionary work in the colonies. In the twentieth century, when Irish immigration slowed down, this source still for much of the church's hierarchy has emphasized the division between laity and clergy, and prevented clerical life from being seen as a 'normal' destination for Catholic youth. It has also meant that Scottish Catholicism has many of the features of Irish Catholicism, authoritarianism and indifference to the arts, sexual prudery and puritanism combined with a certain tolerance of drunkenness and violence. But Catholicism in Scotland has never focused on the Celtic culture of Scotland as an object specially worthy of protection.

Roman Catholicism in Scotland was ignored in the important 1872 Education Act which settled elementary schooling on a basis more suited to the new, urbanized society than was the old parochial school system. The Act did not provide for denominational schools but by insisting that religious education should take place and leaving it to local boards to decide the flavour of this education, it gave opportunities for the schooling to be overtly Protestant. There are enough nineteenth-century instances of Poor Law authorities acting in the interests of Protestant proselytisation to explain the unwillingness of the Catholic population to use the state system until the 1918 Act made possible a denominational system. But in some areas efforts were made before this to provide a Catholic teaching staff in areas exclusively Roman Catholic. There is an interesting account of the life of such a Catholic teacher in South Uist in the 1880s, sent there by the efforts of Catholic societies. His personal religious impact can, in fact, have been very slight, for he spoke no Gaelic and made no effort to learn any. His attitude to the local population was like that of a member of the British establishment in India to the people of a remote hill tribe: kindly, sympathetic and curious but totally uninvolved.[1] His mission is an instance of the values of the late nineteenth century. Religion had a high priority but was not seen in any social or cultural context. The 1918 Act allowed a full provision of schools under Catholic management, but left little option to parents as to whether they wished to be separated off from Protestant neighbours in this facility. Religious justice was achieved by perpetuating social division.

The Irish who came to Scotland in the nineteenth century merged as fully as religion allowed. They did not, on the whole, bring over the political linkages of Ireland or form special political pressure groups as in America. This may have been because of wise leadership by their priesthood. It may also have been because coming in to fill the poorest jobs in the labour market their time was taken up with survival. As a large proportion of the immigrants were Protestants from the north, the Irish in Scotland would not be expected to speak with a united voice about Irish affairs. The migration did directly add to the sectarian nature of nineteenth-century Scotland.

Splits also divided Protestantism into hostile groups, and the unpopularity of movements for reunion shows that there were more than the ostensible differences in theology keeping Christian opposed to Christian. The various churches had their territories clearly marked out, socially or geographically. The United Presbyterians were, for instance, the way of faith for the small but successful tradesman, Episcopalianism for the landed gentry, the Church of Scotland for the agricultural labourer.[2]

There were trends, in spite of the apparent divisions within the churches, which were general. One was the failure of all Protestant organizations to reach down into the mass of the unskilled working class in the towns. The established church might hold on to the farm labourer, though some part of the apparent hold came from the fact that many labourers moved around too frequently for their failure to attend church to lead to the removal of their names from the roll. But it had little contact with labour in the big towns.[3] The basic features of Protestant ideas about society were in various ways either unattainable or actually unattractive to working people. Presbyterian churches stressed the need for education and Bible study, a severe sexual code, financial solvency and in many cases abstinence from alcohol, the restriction of Sunday activity and regular appearances in church in respectable clothes. In 1851 a census of church attendance produced some inflated figures which suggested that about half the country's population might go to church. All sorts of reasons have been given to explain the certain absence of the other half, and since the figures were inflated there is more than this to explain. Religion wrapped round the cities but did not enter into many parts of them.

Among those who did belong to churches there was a changing social relationship. Less and less in the big cities could a congregation be a real community, but community identification was weak in much of the countryside too. Liturgical and disciplinary practices emphasized this. There was a retreat from activities of the congregation as a whole. Baptism was often private. Prayer had always in the presbyterian churches had a larger role for instruction of the congregation than of communion with God. When in the 1870s it became accepted in the established church that hymn singing was not a prohibited activity, and organs were introduced to churches, the internal planning of the buildings often made it necessary to place the organ as the central object in front of the congregation. Geographically as well as institutionally the churches appeared a society of professionals confronting a society of citizens. In some highland parishes the anti-social concept of the function of the church had gone even further. It was regarded as a great achievement, for instance, that Roderick Macleod, Minister in Bracadale, had reduced the parish communion roll from 250 to less than ten.[4] Doubtless when it stood at 250 some semi-pagans were still included among the believers. But at under ten it meant the leadership by a narrow, self-perpetuating oligarchy and the acceptance that church life was only for those fully conscious of righteousness. Highland communities preferred the extreme Calvinist and more austere of the divisions of nineteenth-century presbyterianism, and made a core of membership within those churches totally opposed to the intellectual and social currents of the time. Free Church leaders might groan about the fanaticism of the Highlands: that it could so easily be stirred up was a common complaint of Principal Rainy.[5] But it was initially the creation of the same men and ethos which had made the Disruption. That the Free Church had difficulty in dealing with this attitude came from other intellectual trends it had encouraged and was slow to turn against, in particular the belief, itself not founded in Scripture, that no activities were 'lawful' if they could not be shown to be based on Scripture, and that the Bible was directly the inspired word of God. In 1880, long after churches all over the world had recognized that the sources of biblical inspiration were, at the very least, complex, a considerable section of the Free Church was trying to prosecute Professor Robertson Smith for suggesting that God was not the author of certain books in the Old Testament.[6]

Scotland's churches continued to occupy a more important place in the life of the nation in the twentieth century than was the case in many other countries. The Roman Catholic communion has attempted a stranglehold on part of the school system. The General Assemblies of the free and established churches have played a part in political expression. Even after the belated reunion of much of presbyterian Scotland in and after 1929 the surviving dissentient Free Church has received publicity for its views which neither its intellects nor its membership has justified. Churchgoing, whether for genuinely religious or for social conformist reasons, has retained a hold on many more than in most parts of Europe.

But this continuation of influence has been combined with intellectual loss. The churches have little influence on literature or the arts in the twentieth century. The established church has kept up membership largely by sinking dogma, so that by the mid-twentieth century hardly a word of the Calvinism of the Westminster Confession, still nominally the expression of its belief, was to be heard in many of its Sunday schools or sermons. This would not matter if the dogmatic statements of the seventeenth century had been replaced by a more acute christological understanding, a more sophisticated appreciation of the nature of biblical authority and a sharper realization of the problems of man in society. Individual ministries have supplied these wants, but not the church as a whole in any standard or statement generally acceptable. The dissenting churches have held to older dogma at the expense of ignoring the problems of the twentieth century, and by methods of discipline and exclusion which have alienated most people of youth or enterprise. The price of church membership figures has been high in terms of social relevance.

The Sportsman's Scotland

Even before the mid-nineteenth century, moneyed and idle men came to Scotland for the pleasure of killing. Thornton's memoirs, an amalgam of various trips in the late eighteenth and early nineteenth centuries, show the attraction of the more accessible parts of the Highlands for a man with a rifle or shotgun, money and time. The native aristocracy had enjoyed shooting and eating game throughout the eighteenth century, and had therefore taken some care for its protection. A stream of irritable conflict exists in baron court records over the habit of the peasantry of burning the old heather on the moors to improve the pasture, and doing it late in the spring, so that it disturbed the nesting of the moor fowl. The practice was legal only early in the year, but the law was constantly flouted, and men prosecuted for 'muirburn'. In the nineteenth century improved gun power and the withdrawal of tacksmen and lesser landowners from close involvement in the daily work of organizing farming, presented more people with the leisure and opportunities of men like Thornton. Game was more carefully preserved, and wild life which did not count as game became scarcer. Osgood Mackenzie's memoir, *A Hundred Years in the Highlands*, which spans the nineteenth century, starting with memories from his mother and uncles, gives a sharp impression of this process. MacKenzie had a gun from the age of nine and for over 60 years blazed away at anything that moved. By his 70s he was recording that several species, such as the pine marten, had disappeared. 'My mother used to have an average of forty or fifty skins of martens brought to her by the keepers every year. . .The pine martens, the polecats and the badgers are all quite extinct.'

The cultivation of game not only made for a less rich native fauna. It encouraged the exclusion of the people at large from the reservoirs of wild life, and as the construction of highland railways proceeded in the 1860s and after, the exclusion of the native highland population for the benefit of those from outside who could pay for expensive recreation. A satirical picture of this is to be found in the description of the shooting lodge of Crummie-Toddie in Trollope's novel *The Duke's Children*: 'Everything had been made to give way to deer and game... There was hardly a potato patch left in the district, nor a head of cattle to be seen. There were no inhabitants remaining, or so few that they could be absorbed in game-preserving or cognate duties.' The tenant was described as regarding Crummie-Toddie as 'the nearest thing to Paradise on earth'; all that it needed was a clause in the lease 'against the making of any new roads, opening of footpaths or building of bridges'.

This was intended as exaggeration; Trollope's acquaintaince with Scotland was not intimate. Yet this does not really misrepresent the way that, by the 1870s, the native population was being pushed to one side for the pleasures of the rich incomers. At least Thornton had had to share the countryside with its people.

The highland population had, in many parts, been 'cleared' from the inland straths and so from using the inland hills as rough grazing. Instead these hills had become sheep farms. Trollope implies that the people had been cleared away for game, but every scrap of factual evidence points against this.[7] Clearance was always for sheep farming, with the development of 'industries' and fishing on the coasts to provide new work and support for the people. But the industries were unsuccessful, and eventually in the 1870s wool prices began to decline.

Upland fertility had already been expended in the sheep grazing.

The great 'wool rents' which had been paid mid-century for sheep farms would clearly never come again. With the rapid collapse of sheep farming landowners turned much of the higher land into the only thing that would still bring in high rents, deer forest. The Highlands were now accessible enough to provide long holiday homes for southern families, the sporting rifle made deer shooting a skilled and less haphazard sport, and the new middle-class life provided people in search of holidays. Grouse shooting and salmon fishing added to the value of highland property. It was these activities, all requiring large amounts of money and near empty countryside, which Scotland came to stand for in the eyes of the fashionable world. If such features were to be marketable, the continued exclusion of the local population from the inland straths was necessary. Gillies, gamekeepers, gardeners and occasional shepherds, became the people tolerated in the sportsmen's paradise. The holiday households often brought with them from the south their domestic labour force. If they needed skilled services such as the work of outside craftsmen they sent away for them to nearby towns. At the same time a humbler strain of tourism, of people who could not afford to take a shooting lodge for a whole summer, led to the creation of the new towns and villages that follow the railways into the Highlands, burgeoning with Gothic hotels — Pitlochry, Kingussie, Nethybridge, Dornoch. Golf, as it became fashionable, added a new use of good land. Tourism accentuated the natural economic tendency of population to concentrate in towns and villages rather than spread about the glens.

This process was much less marked in the outer and northern islands. As railway and road replaced coastal steamer as the main method of long distance communication — the advantages of this change can be seen in Philip Gaskell's account of the use of a Morvern estate as holiday home for a London banking family[8] — the difference in accessibility between mainland and island became conspicuous. In the Long Island and the Northern Isles clearance was less marked: a denser population remained in the townships, mixing poor farming with under-capitalized and therefore over-dangerous fishing, or taking service in the merchant navy and with whalers. In the case of the Northern Isles this less traumatic development may relate to a less urgent demographic situation. The population growth there had been slower from the late eighteenth century, partly at least because a pattern of temporary and permanent emigration of young men kept the sex ratio so distorted that over a third of the women had no prospect of marriage. The material relics which still survive in Shetland and Orkney suggest that the threat of subsistence crisis was less imminent than on the mainland and in the Western Isles. It may also be that the Norse strain in Lewis and the far north produced a population with greater capacity of resistance to outward pressure, or rather one relying less on apparent passivity. At any rate by the twentieth century the Norse areas show special vigour of local life and culture, and also less depopulation, than the Celtic. Depopulation and clearance did more than simply shift people around: in many places they took the mainspring out of local culture.

In spite of the fact that 'clearance' had not been for game, this was how it came to be regarded in that unreliable but revealing strand of evidence, folk memory, and this was how it was retailed to lowland Scotland. Crofting townships, over-crowded on the coastal strips and menaced by the risk of deer breaking through into the farmland from the hill, rethought their past in terms of the current resentment and formulated myth. Myths as well as facts are important in historical development.

Depopulation of the Highlands in the mid-Victorian period was voluntary as well as enforced. The standard of living in visible material matters, such as housing, food, money to spend, was much higher in the towns than in the crofting townships, and information about it spread back through the people who had already gone to town, so that many moved away for it. The cultural loss was less obvious: so were the risks to health of urban life, or the waves of unemployment which could bring families into destitution and destruction. The cost of the move to the lowland towns for the early twentieth century is vividly shown in Edwin Muir's autobiography.[9] Tuberculosis, to which highlanders in the past had not been exposed and so were especially susceptible, hit the immigrant population. Temporary migrants brought it back to the crofting townships where it took a terrible toll.[10]

In the 1880s, when there still remained in many areas settlements more dense than the agricultural capacity of the land could fully support, notably in Skye and the northern tip of Lewis, the land law was changed to give the crofter what soon became absolute, inherited security for his smallholding. The crofts, still not large enough to support a household, had already come to be used as partial support only. Men went away to distant fishing or harvest work for much of the summer to remove their appetites from the family's supplies and to earn the cash which paid the rent. This was not new. In the eighteenth century the highlander harvest worker had been an important part of the farm system of lowland Scotland. But now the pattern was often to work in the towns, and for longer than the mere harvest season. The results were damaging to the farming standards of the Highlands, where those left behind could not keep the land in good condition; to health because of tuberculosis in the returning population; and to society generally because of social distortion. The crofts gradually became places to which the old retired, visited by their active descendants for a short time in the year, perhaps also rearing the generation of children, but not providing a balanced community. This type of society was particularly prone to a fanatic conservatism in religion, which in turn ensured that youths, as they grew up, would get out to find freedom. There was a steady drain of physical strength and personal enterprise.

So, not only did highland population continue to fall, but it became distorted. Again the Norse areas did better than the Celtic. In Lewis the weaving of tweed, in Orkney better land and in Shetland fishing and whaling, all combined to hold a higher proportion of young adults for at least part of the year. In the mid-twentieth century the extension of tourism down the social scale at last brought new ways of earning money within the Highlands, while a belated recognition that Gaelic culture existed and had contributions to make to the whole of Scotland led to greater government effort to revify the highland economy. At last the formal machine of schooling was persuaded to stop repressing the native language. The 1872 Education Act set up large, relatively expensive (and ugly) schools in which the local children were punished for speaking in their native language. The repression of the language was not built into the Act, and was expressly refuted in legislation of 1878, but it was a natural component of the professional approach of the lowland-trained teachers and of the school inspectors on which much of the schools grant depended. In some places, for instance Ness in Lewis, the local community reacted with passive resistance, by refusing to send the children to school whenever it was inconvenient. It was alleged that they could not go to school in winter without shoes.[11] Poor attendance figures cut into the government grant, and increased the local cost of the school, and the local resentment. Not till after the Second World War did the societies ostensibly devoting themselves to the preservation of what they considered to be Gaelic culture turn from folk song and poetry to the unromantic hard work of enabling Gaelic children to have textbooks and teaching curricula in their own language. By then radio was already a source of the English tongue in most homes. Soon it would be reinforced by the visual impact of television. The retreat of Gaelic continued.

The 1872 Act ensured that, by the 1920s, English was understood and spoken through almost the whole of the Highlands. This gave further openings for the drain of young people to jobs elsewhere. Scholastic proficiency of an old-fashioned kind, the route to the Scottish universities, was a route to the professions too, and taken by many, for the population was highly intelligent. Some, but not many, came back after training, to practise their professional skills in the Highlands. There were not many jobs to come back to. On the whole formal education did little to enrich the life of those who chose to stay in the Highlands, and much to destroy their respect for their native language.

Scotland, the Land of Poverty

Nobody would have used this title for Scotland as a whole in the late nineteenth century. Standards of living were then much lower than those enjoyed by developed nations today, but they were then higher than in many parts of Europe, and certainly higher than in Scotland's own past. Only in the Highlands was poverty the striking feature. Many parts of the industrialized and industrializing world had populations living lives skimped in nourishment, lacking in recreation, starved of opportunity and cut short by accident and disease. Within the British Isles the rural Lowlands of Scotland ranked as a 'high wage' area, though even the highest rural wages meant a hard and meagre living. The wages were 'high' because it was relatively easy for labour to move from farm to town, and town wages had been 'high' for some time. Many of the farm workers in central and north-east Scotland had to leave farm work when they married, for in those areas farming made little use of the work of women and children, and consequently the pressure by the farmers was for a labour force mostly of young, unmarried men.[12] Some of this labour was housed in 'bothies'.

A government investigation in the 1890s described these bothies as 'very rude dwellings' and the whole system as 'a disgrace to Scotland'. It was by then assumed that at least ten hours work made up a normal day: longer would be demanded of those caring for cattle. A ploughman in Caithness, where the wages were lowest, would earn £36 a year, if he kept fit, and this was better than the 12s. a week of southern England. In Lanarkshire he would get as much as £52. His day would start at five, he would have got his horses to the field by six, and would bring them back to the stable for their and his dinner at eleven. They would be back in the fields at one and stay till six. He then had to groom and feed them before he went home. But where he was free of the bothy system, and provided his wife kept rigorously to the old style of housekeeping, with very little money spent on wheat bread, tea or meat, his diet would be adequate.[13]

Even without bothies, there is at this date a stream of criticism of Scottish rural housing. Much of it was damp and cramped, lacked cupboard space and other indoor conveniences, and in most places sanitation meant outside privies, often called 'ashpits', shared with several families.

The relative prosperity of rural Scotland is shown by complaints about the difficulty of getting women workers on the farms in many areas. Young women had grown up to dislike farm work, and where they could, left home for more attractive jobs. We can see why when we read the description of the dress of 'bondagers', the women workers of the Borders. These 'warp wisps of straw round their legs to well up the calf, then pin the back and front of short warm petticoats together,' 'to save appearance'. Victorian ideas of decency did not equip a girl for farm labour, and this was before the days of cheap weather-proof fabrics. We have a later picture of these bondagers in the early twentieth century using sacks to keep the rain off their heads and backs.[14]

In 1893 it was stated that farm wages had risen by 50% in the past half-century, a rise sharper than in most other occupations. Women's share of this, however, remained unfairly low in relation to men's, and when women demanded more, farmers would turn to Irish labour instead. Wages, as quoted, were often nominal. In many parts of the country workers still preferred to be paid partly in kind. The predominance of mixed farming in Scotland meant that there were not many areas where the basic elements of a balanced diet were lacking. Milk products abounded. But not all milk was good milk, and the shift in taste in food was away from some of the older and safer types of it. Buttermilk was becoming less popular: it had been described as a staple element in the diet of both town and country in the 1860s.[15] 'Sweet' milk, that is milk unsoured and therefore a good breeding ground for bacteria, was pleasanter and more sustaining. Almost all the cattle of the main dairy counties of the Lowlands were riddled with tuberculosis. The newly available wheat flour became roller ground, with most of the germ, and therefore the protein and vitamin B complex, removed. All the same the most sensitive indicator of living conditions, the mortality rates of infants and young children, compared well at the end of the nineteenth century with those of other countries. If 30s. a week seems poor pay for the skill and strength of a farm labourer, it kept his family fed, and his work was on six-month contracts which freed him from the constant terror of unemployment. It is a healthy sign of this class of workmen that farmers were complaining in the late nineteenth century that the men were becoming resentful of long hours, ready to break away to other jobs, even at the cost of broken contracts. They would not allow their wages to be cut in the long agricultural depression. In East Lothian they could obtain work at 4s. a day as caddies on the new golf links, altogether a pleasanter and easier task than farming, and so the farmers had to raise wages.

It is much harder to gain a clear picture of what was happening in the late nineteenth century to urban wages. We know that the jute industry, by then the dominant activity of Dundee, was one of the worst paid in Britain, and with a high susceptibility to the business cycle and so a high risk of unemployment. The most recent historian of the Glasgow area suggests that in the late nineteenth century wages there were advancing as fast as in industrial England.[16] The ship-building and engineering achievements of the Clyde had made it a centre of skilled workmen, and it continued to hold this high reputation until the First World War. But the level of wages is only part of the answer to the question of the level of incomes. We are still in the dark about the frequency and level of unemployment in the nineteenth century, but we do know that the type of industry found by the Clyde was one with a strong tendency to cyclical unemployment. The demand for ships happens only for short periods at the top of world booms. The shipbuilding firms needed a large pool of skilled labour which they could use for these short periods only. Family incomes may also have been held down by a lack of the lighter jobs which can be done by women and boys. The Irish labour force filled the niche of the unskilled and low-paid labouring jobs. There is reason to doubt whether high wages was the whole of the picture.

Traditions of poverty, rapid industrialization and the financial insecurity of the aristocracy of skilled labour may partly explain the most characteristic feature of late nineteenth-century urban life, the low standard of housing, but they do not do so fully. Numerous comments and descriptions exist from the last 20 years of the nineteenth century, evidence that housing had come to the fore as a social problem. Housing can be inadequate in solidity of structure, space available or sanitary features. Scottish urban housing failed on the last two counts and the rural on all three.[17] The early sanitary movement of the 1850s and 1860s had concentrated on providing some sort of urban sewerage and good water supply. In the 1860s

Glasgow was regarded as a pioneer in this, an enterprising city because it had, by tapping the waters of Loch Katrine, plentiful pure water. Its achievement was rewarded by the slight impact only of the cholera epidemic of 1866. But a host of other killer diseases remained; typhoid (far harder to stamp out than cholera), summer diarrhoea of children, measles and whooping cough.[18] Even smallpox, which could by then have been eliminated, staged a large scale revival in the 1870s which at least secured full obedience to the law on compulsory vaccination. Legislation empowering town authorities to take action about 'nuisances' and overcrowding was piece-meal and there was not a co-ordinated system of local government, even after the major Public Health Act of 1867. Even when towns had adequate powers, as from the Act of 1880 which allowed much more positive action and permitted the towns to act as landlords, they did not necessarily use them. The City Engineer of Greenock admitted in 1884 that he had not heard of an important Act of 16 years before.[19] Local government was run by a few overworked officials and such gaps in their knowledge should not be a surprise. But if the officials did not act, then only individuals could, and tenement life in its closeness made it difficult for people to present their near neighbours to the courts as creators of nuisance.

City authorities in Scotland were prepared to use their powers of demolition, and were proceeding against the special form of housing most disapproved of, the closed court. But they were unwilling to take positive steps to provide alternatives, or to recognize that demolition usually merely increased the overcrowding in some other insalubrious tenement. We have no certain knowledge of the levels of overcrowding in the 1860s and 1870s because the census officials had not yet made up their minds whether a flat in a tenement was or was not a 'house'. But in the 1880s it is clear that it was severe, with over 24% of Glasgow's families living in single rooms. By 1884 Edinburgh had demolished 13,000 'houses', often single rooms, and Glasgow had got rid of 30,000 and was planning an attack on a further 20,000. The displacement, some of it the result of railway building, had, it was claimed, scattered 'the vicious and criminal population' of certain central areas. Criminal populations are not so easily broken up. A Glasgow baillie assured an investigating Royal Commission that the people had been able to squeeze into nearby houses without hardship. Perhaps it would have been truer to say without expressed hardship. There was a striking absence of working-class pressure for better housing, and a working-class acceptance that all the city could be expected to do about overcrowding was to penalize the victims. Lodgers abounded in the single-room houses. The city of Glasgow took the policy of 'ticketing' these and other small flats with the maximum number of people permitted to live in them, on the basis of 300 cubic feet to an adult. Raids were made in the dead of night to see who was there, driving the surplus population to a refugee existence on the roof. In Dundee the permitted level of space was set at only just above 200 cubic feet per head. Middle-class opinion was not ready to accept having to pay for the housing of other classes, and organized working-class opinion, for instance the Trades Council of Edinburgh, was not ready to think of socialist provision. There was even considerable hesitation over the idea that the Council of Edinburgh should provide lighting and control the state of the common stairs of the tenements. In Glasgow the common stairs were described as 'practically urinals', and so they would remain while there were no more convenient means of relief. For Dundee it was stated that those who could find houses of two rooms would gladly pay the extra rent for the space, but elsewhere it was held that the lower paid workers would not. Edinburgh at least was well provided with better housing which the skilled artisans could afford.[20]

One important feature of the Scottish way of life could be used to justify inaction on housing and on other evils. This was drink. It was always possible for middle-class citizens to point out that the money spent on drink by many in the cities could have enabled them to be more spaciously housed, though it would not have dealt with the physical problems of inserting sanitary equipment into massive stone-built tenements. Certainly drink expenditure masked the issue of how adequate working-class incomes might be. Scottish levels of consumption and Scottish drinking patterns were not social but aimed at oblivion.

There is good reason to think that many in the cities were underfed, both in the nineteenth century and the early twentieth. Nutritional levels, better then than in the late eighteenth century, were low in fats and protein. There was still little scientific knowledge, and it is clear that those who attempted to advise the poor on expenditure did not understand enough, scientifically or socially, to be much help. A group of doctors looking into the food of the poor in Edinburgh in 1902 suggested that 'in the dietaries of the poorer classes the fats should be cut down as much as possible and the energy should, as far as the digestion will allow, be supplied in carbohydrates'. They went on to lament recent changes: 'the reasons of the disuse of porridge is to be found in the lazy habits of the labouring classes'.[20] On the carbohydrate issue the poor knew better than their betters that they needed something else, and if on a largely carbohydrate diet, and not enough of that, they were lazy, sympathy would seem more appropriate than disapproval. It was unreasonable to expect this section of society to reduce an already inadequate diet to pay for better housing, and if the response of such people was to seek the quick way out of alcohol, one should not be surprised.

It is sometimes claimed that the housing failure in Scotland was the result of the tremendous urban growth of the nineteenth century. This is only partly true. The rural areas and the mining districts show that low standards were well established. In any case Scottish cities, though they grew fast, did not do so throughout the nineteenth century. Their most rapid growth was early in the century. The fact that most of Scotland built in stone rather than brick made building expensive, but also helped it to be secure and permanent. It has been suggested that one reason for the lack of good working-class houses in Glasgow was the building of the middle-class suburbs in the later nineteenth century.[21] But this is to argue that the building industry could not increase its labour force. It also ignores the fact that, compared to most European cities, Glasgow has a relatively small middle-class population.

The Scottish pattern of tall tenements, many of which can still be seen in older parts of cities such as Dundee, is sometimes attributed to the continuation of a feudal land law, but it seems sounder to credit it to the general urban tradition, for it is to be found in older unindustrialized burghs. In Inveraray, for instance, it dictates the whole character of the little town. The development of Glasgow seems also to suggest that this was what the urban population liked, for when the big engineering and shipbuilding works had been constructed on the outskirts of the old city, the workers continued to live in the centre. The pattern of movement to work was, by modern ideas, inside out, with the workers streaming out at dawn to work, and coming at home at night to the centre.

The enquiries in the late nineteenth and early twentieth centuries into housing problems reveal more significant reasons for the failure than any technical matter such as the size of the labour force, the material used or the land law in the gulf in the ways of life between the classes and in the failure of those who governed the cities to understand the point of view of the mass of people who lived in them. The tone of replies to questions suggests that the officials of the city treated its workers as another species. It also seems that, for some time at least in the nineteenth century, the urban working class was prepared to acquiesce in the narrow bounds of self-expression and the reduced sense of community spirit allowed.

It is surely not without significance that Scotland can claim the worst of the notorious band of bad poets of the nineteenth century in William McGonagall, the Dundee handloom weaver. McGonagall's aesthetic and verbal limitations were displayed in the first poem he ever wrote, in praise of a local minister. He was 47 years old and he wrote, he claimed, under sudden inspiration:

> The first time I heard him speak,
> 'Twas in the Kinnaird Hall,
> Lecturing on the Garibaldi movement
> As loud as he could bawl.

But his special poetical touch is not his appalling prosody but his emotional inadequacy, which gives the reader of his poems the frequent sense of having slipped on a literary banana skin.

> Fellow citizens of Dundee
> Isn't it really very nice
> To think of James Scrymgeour trying
> To rescue fallen creatures from the paths of vice?

This sort of thing happens often because of his special devotion to the description of local disasters.

> And he gave one half frantic leap, with his heart full of woe
> And came down upon the roof of a public house twenty feet below . . .

This is not simply the result of a badly informed, self-educated man who normally spoke Scots trying to write in alien and acceptable English. If that were all one could admire it. It is the work of a deprived personality who does not really feel emotions but registers the expected reaction.

The social problems of poverty and overcrowding, already the source of concern on the eve of the First World War, became conspicuous during the inter-war period of economic failure. Those parts of Scotland already lagging in poverty, such as Dundee, lapsed further into misery and Clydeside, once renowned for skill and good wages, became settled in unemployment and depression. The rural labourers were better off in material terms than they had been in the past, but this meant no great standard of living, and economic dislocation cast into insecurity the class of small farmers. By the 1930s Scotland's once relatively good health statistics had failed to improve at the rate of those of other countries, and were among the worst in Europe. This was particularly a cause for shame, or should have been, because the country boasted of several distinguished medical schools and hospitals, educating in them a large proportion of the medical profession for work in other countries. Only late in the 1930s did there develop pressure in the various branches of government to do something about the matter. House building, infant and maternal mortality, tuberculosis, at last became the topic of special enquiries and special efforts. The results began to show during the Second World War. Infant mortality, for instance, which had fallen slowly since the turn of the century, was halved in less than a decade in the 1940s. Tuberculosis figures, which were beginning to rise just before the war, were reduced to negligible levels in the 1950s with the new weapons of modern chemistry.

There was treatment, then, of the social aspects of what had become a relatively poor part of the United Kingdom, but not so completely of the economic causes of this relative poverty. Some of these causes are probably deeply embedded in the Scottish social ethos. The country has prided itself for several generations on producing professional men, lawyers, bankers and doctors. It has not given the same general respect to the career of entrepreneur, even though individual entrepreneurs have at times made great names. The social strength of the country seems to lie in producing a disciplined and closely ordered middle class with high standards of personal integrity, rather than in simply making money.

This middle class was not closed. Scottish educational provision throughout the nineteenth century created openings by which children, or rather boys, of any social level, if able and intellectually docile, could pass through to higher education. Even the 1872 Education Act, passed when Scottish institutions were most influenced by the sister country England, differed from the English contemporary legislation in insisting that state education was offered to the entire child population, not merely to the working class, and in maintaining these openings. There were fee-paying schools hinged on to the state system in a way which provided the advantages of selective education at a low proportion of its true cost to many middle-class families, and into such schools a trickle, later a small stream, of children from working-class families who saw education as the route to advancement, would pass. Class divisions were as sharp as anywhere in western Europe, but some element of upward mobility was not incompatible with them. Neither the way up for 'the lad o' pairts' (not of course for his sister), nor the absence of class accents in most of Scotland should be taken as evidence that Scotland was a classless society. Rather it should be seen as a society in which the function of class was clearly defined and understood and, in one or two particular ways, limited. The route from school to the local university was open to a considerable number of adolescents by the twentieth century, and the cost of attendance there was within the range of many pockets. The Scottish universities retained for long a rather dogmatic and 'schoolmarmish' quality in their methods of teaching and the type of thought which they endeavoured to promote, stemming from a closeness to the requirements of a large part of the community. In a secular sense they were carrying out the role that Knox had laid down for them in the sixteenth century. These features gave way slowly in the face of new types of knowledge and thinking. In some ways the twentieth-century move from pedagogy to research was a repeat of that of the eighteenth century.

Scotland the Reprobate

Perhaps it has been a necessary result of the long adherence to the sharp Calvinist dichotomy between the elect and the reprobate, as well as the strength of the forces of evil, that Scotland should long have manifested features which dismayed the social observers of the day. The discovery in the 1850s that Scotland had a percentage of illegitimate births far higher (it was mistakenly thought) than most of western Europe, and certainly higher than England's, caused dismay, and this dismay was enhanced by the particular location of the areas of high illegitimacy. These were certain rural districts, where the corrupting effects of the big cities, of modern life, and even of radical literature, could hardly be given the blame. North-east Scotland, particularly Banffshire, had, and continued well into the twentieth century, to have startlingly high levels of illegitimacy, yet this was an area of good educational provision, strong family bonds and relatively good wages. In the south-west, the old covenanting base, the figures were nearly as high, and here the trouble could not be blamed, as most things were, on Irish incomers, because all observers were struck with the relative chasteness of the Irish working class.[22] In 1895 the poor law inspector of Torthorwald parish, Dumfriesshire, was protesting about the unfair burden placed on parish funds by illegitimacy. Girls went out from the parish to work as farm servants elsewhere, and he felt that these other places should share in the burden of an illegitimacy percentage of 30, high even for the south-west.[23] It has recently been

suggested that the high illegitimacy levels are signs of the continuation of a working class sub-culture with a different scale of
values from that which had come to dominate middle-class views.[24]
With the nineteenth-century religious obsession on sexual morals as
more important than other aspects of morality — there are frequent
references to the illegitimacy rate as a touchstone of the morality of a
country — we must see that this sub-culture deeply disturbed middle-
class moralists. It was as worrying to the nineteenth century as
Scotland's twentieth-century reputation for violent crime is today.

Crime is the area of social record where it is hardest to make
comparative use of figures. These depend on changing definitions of
crime, on the vigour of police activity and on public co-operation
with that activity. But even allowing for these sources of doubt,
modern Scotland has achieved an unenviable reputation for violence. The crime rate in Glasgow and Dundee is higher than in other
British cities, homicide in the country as a whole is markedly more
frequent than in many other countries. Assaults by married men on
their wives and children, often but not always when in liquor, are
taken for granted as part of domestic life in many families. Football
hooliganism, regarded by English social critics as a manifestation of
the 1960s, has been conspicuous in Glasgow for over half a
century. Far too little is known in general about the social origins of
crime for it to be profitable to look for social explanations of
Scotland's special position in it, but it seems likely that the polarization forced on men's minds by Calvinism may have played a
part in the past and that in the twentieth century the architectural
inhumanity of much of the material environment of the cities may
have also contributed. In many areas 'improved' housing has
created communities in which community spirit is almost
unattainable.

There is also, again, the role of alcohol. Patterns of drink in
Scotland have certainly contributed to violence as they have to
poverty and ill health. But in this matter there is certainly no simple
relationship. The most drunken areas of Scotland, the north and
north-west, are not the ones with the highest crime figures.

In the twentieth century the attack on drunkenness has proceeded
by raising the price of alcohol and limiting the times and places
where it can be obtained. This attack started with the Temperance
Act of 1913, which allowed areas where there was a strong antipathy
to alcohol among the majority of the voters to forbid the issue of
licences to public houses, and so pass the problem of their own
drinking minority to other areas. Before this could take effect
wartime restrictions of hours and wartime taxation had cut into the

drinking pattern of Scotland and brought the weekly cases of 'drunk and disorderly' down by a significant amount. In the inter-war period the proliferation of alternative recreations further reduced the amount of orgiastic drinking. But lowering of the level of uncontrolled drinking has not been accompanied by a lowering of the general level of violence.

The problem of drink in Scotland is not simply a problem of drinking but also of extreme opposition to it. It is the polarization of opinion on this issue which is as destructive of social harmony as the effects of drunkenness, and probably this polarization explains the fact that whereas the amount of alcohol consumed in Scotland over the year as a whole is not particularly high by general European standards, the Scots consume it in a way which makes the level of drunkenness high. In the 1960s a Scotsman was six times as likely to die of alcoholism as an Englishman. Polarization over alcohol tends to accentuate the gulf in Scotland between the recreational activities permissible in the two sexes, yet even so Scottish women are twice as likely to die of drink as English women. These figures are probably more revealing than comparisons of arrests for drunkenness, since such arrests depend on the tolerance of the police, which may well vary between countries. Among the unpleasant results of Scotland's drinking habits stands alienation between the sexes, as well as muddled theological thinking and hypocrisy.

Scottish Democracy

This image is one much favoured by Scots for themselves. Like all such images, the idea that Scotland has been in some individual way especially democratic holds a grain of truth. For the last century or more the ostensible politics of Scotland have stood to the left of those of the rest of the United Kingdom. But this has often been in name rather than in fact. In the 1880s Scotland sent to Parliament a large quota of Liberal members, but demanded little through them that would have been of benefit to the whole country. The geographical, religious and social divisions of Scotland's population would, in any case, have made a meaningful radical policy difficult to devise. There was pressure for disestablishment of the church among those who belonged to other communions, and for changes in the land law to benefit tenantry, but little for anything which would affect the quality of life for the ordinary urbanized or industrial Scot. The socialist movement which eventually produced the twentieth-century's Labour party owed a great deal to individual Scots, but for a long time did badly in Scotland itself. Keir Hardie, for instance, was defeated in his homeland, and had to represent a Welsh constituency when he brought Labour into Parliament. Eventually he turned his attention more to international than to even British politics. Other hopeful working-class politicians also had to go south to get elected. Yet the left wing these men represented had by the end of the Edwardian peace produced a proliferation of socialist and communist organizations on Clydeside. Their existence and strength were probably a consequence of the special hardship of trade-cycle fluctuations there. The movement had strong trade union links, sustained at least one powerful newspaper, *Forward*, but was slow to be heard in Parliament. The war gave the unions a chance to be heard on national issues. It was in Glasgow that the stresses produced by the war, particularly rising prices and rents with stationary wages, produced the disturbances and resistance which eventually forced the government to pay attention to the demands of the working class. Rent restriction, a hand-to-mouth response to part of the problem, entered into with no recognition of its deplorable long-term results, was part of the response. More significantly the Clyde workers started up the resistance to attempts to impose industrial conscription in the cause of patriotism, and went on from there to take a part in the syndicalist 'shop stewards' movement. Syndicalism was not a clear-headed nor an effective creed, but when united with the resistance to wartime organization could give apparent unity and purpose to a widespread discontent. With peace, the inherent inadequacy of the philosophy and the determined hostility of organized trade union-ism to shop floor control broke up the movement. But its strength had already waned in Scotland. The sectional nature of the movement, dependent solely on skilled workers in a few trades in a necessarily fragmented industry, engineering, kept its appeal nar-row.

Syndicalism died but was followed by a political development on the Clyde which certainly benefited from the angry purposefulness which had informed it. This is the manifestation known as the 'Red Clyde'. In 1922 a body of left-wing Labour members, many of them also members of the old Independent Labour Party of Keir Hardie, came to Parliament from the Clyde. For a time they made the I.L.P. an influential 'ginger group' within the Labour party. Half the I.L.P. members held Scottish seats, and since Labour had now replaced Liberalism as the dominant party in Scotland and the major party on the left in Britain, the needs of urban Scotland could be placed before Parliament. The men involved felt deeply, and were backed by a proliferation of socialist and communist organizations. It is tempting to see the 'Red Clyde' as a national expression, though it could speak only for the urban core of the nation. But if it was such an expression, it is hard to explain why it did not last. The whole thing fizzled out in the 1930s in a split between I.L.P. and Labour, in recrimination, and partly through personal inadequacy. No appropriate national movement replaced it.

Probably the divisions between different sections of Scottish culture meant that the Clyde could not really speak for Scotland. The east, the north and rural Scotland did not want to take their line from Glasgow. A movement owing much of its vehemence to Marxist rhetoric did not fit easily on to large sections of the people who, if not genuinely religious, liked to retain social conventions based on the religious movements of the nineteenth century. The division on the Clyde itself, between the dominant Protestant skilled working class and the Catholic unskilled, persisted. Much of Catholic concern in local politics went into securing the place of Catholic schools, and much of Labour local activity into the provision of council housing. Housing activities used up energy, and, more seriously, enticed local politicians into vested interests and sometimes corruption. All parties accepted too readily also the division, in practical and political matters, between the sexes. The campaign for votes for women had never found in Scotland the support it gained, for instance, in Lancashire. The churches and the classes united in seeing women as second-class citizens. It is notable that most of the working-class leaders on the left thrown up by Scotland did not succeed in bringing their wives into their movements. Some did not even try. Even Keir Hardie, who strongly supported the women's movement and valued women as political colleagues, did not politicize his wife, and politics estranged the communist and pacifist agitator John Maclean from his. John Wheatley, the most effective of the Clydesiders, and probably the most important contributor to the policy of the 1924 Labour government, kept his wife firmly out of politics. Democracy did not begin at home. In the pre-1914 world, to a lesser extent between the wars, there were a great many strenuous, unpleasant and time-consuming tasks to be done in any house to keep a family fed, cared for, clean and respectable, and in all ranks of society it was assumed that this work was the function of women. For all his political feminism, Keir Hardie was disconcerted when he found himself obliged to cope with the washing up. The pay of Members of Parliament was small, and there was no question of most of the Clydesiders being able to afford a second home in London. Political activity meant constant travel and late night meetings. It was no easy thing to offer to a wife.

Material facts and intellectual weaknesses united to reduce the impact of the left. London was a long way off, and, once there, Glasgow's Members of Parliament became involved in the general disheartening problems of British politics. The Clydesiders failed to use the inter-war depression as an opportunity to stage a major attack on the inadequacies of the relief system in Scotland. 'Poplarism', the attempt to bend the Poor Law to higher standards of support, existed in London, but not where it was more needed, in Glasgow. The parliamentary debates do not show the Clydesiders as particularly well aware of either the social problems of the day or the deeper trends within the country. Inter-war unemployment demoralized the skilled working-class base of the movements of the left. Skilled or unskilled, once unemployed, removal from trade unionism left men with no normal outlet for political activity. Besides this, the prolonged industrial sickness of the great industries of the Clyde produced a spiritual as well as a physical malnutrition. Neither parliamentary democracy through the Labour party nor Marxism gave answers which could easily be applied, and neither managed to seem of real local relevance.

The failure of the 'Red Clyde' was a part of the failure of Labour between the wars, and this was a failure of society as a whole to create a new scale of social priorities. If the inter-war period had a positive democratic achievement it is to be found in the determination created in the minds of working politicians inside and outside Parliament in the Second World War, that these bad times were not to be allowed to come again. The post-war world was to aim at practical amelioration of bad conditions rather than dogmatic statements of policy. Some of the technical progress of the war itself would be used to meet practical needs. The intent was a society more equal in expectation and opportunity. To a considerable degree it was achieved.

That this more equal society meant a great increase eventually in the power of the central government was a price which not all were willing to pay. By the 1950s the Labour party had copied the nineteenth-century Liberals. It relied on Scottish votes to get into power and was in danger of ignoring the Scottish needs which produced these votes. There were obvious discomforts for many parts of Scotland in the new, more flourishing economy. Unemployment, through nowhere near the inter-war level, clung to the same old areas, and for Scotland as a whole was usually twice the general United Kingdom level. The new social service structure of a welfare state fitted the social needs of highland communities badly. New educational opportunities were bought at a high price by scattered rural settlements. No political group was prepared to take on the task of persuading the Scottish people as a whole to be prepared to pay for adequate housing.

The particular result of the problems and discomforts of Scotland's position was the rise of nationalism. Though what Scots wanted to complain of was more the association with Whitehall than the association with England, it was the Scottish National Party which collected the benefit of the complaint. The appeal of this party was mostly to the middle class, but also to the young of all sections. It is yet to be seen whether today's young can think more deeply and represent the country better than did the politicians of the inter-war period.

A new dimension to social democracy came also from an important feature of the new economy, the redistribution of wealth. This has not only been between classes, but also between young people and their parents. By the 1960s it was possible for school leavers to earn enough to support themselves, and very soon to be able to leave home, marry and set up house. Even the wages of women, though they lagged behind those of men, and new chances of work for women, the new structure of jobs which came from the return to work of married women as their children grow up, all these meant a redistribution of the monetary power. In ways not necessarily attractive to those who value traditions of the past, the way has been opened for a more real form of democracy. Nineteenth-century ideas about Scottish democracy applied only to the rights and powers of the fathers of families, but in the 1960s and 70s others have become enfranchised.

Notes

Abbreviations used in the Notes

A.P.S.	*Acts of the Parliaments of Scotland*
B.C.	Bannatyne Club
I.R.	*Innes Review*
M.C.	Maitland Club
N.S.A.	*The New Statistical Account of Scotland*
O.S.A.	*The Statistical Account of Scotland*
N.S.C.	New Spalding Club
P.P.	*Parliamentary Papers*
R.P.Co.	*The Register of the Privy Council*
S.B.R.S.	Scottish Burgh Record Society
S.H.R.	*Scottish Historical Review*
S.H.S.	Scottish History Society
SRO	The Scottish Record Office
S.S.	*Scottish Studies*
S.T.S.	Scottish Text Society

Chapter 1

1. 'Extracts from the kirk session minutes' in W. Cramond, (ed.) *The Records of Elgin* vol II (N.S.C. Aberdeen, 1908), 6 October 1626 and 26 October 1627. By our present calendar both these dates would be ten days later.
2. I am here relying on information from Mrs Jennifer Brown.
3. Dr T.I. Rae has told me of instances of this in the sixteenth century.
4. T.C.Smout, *A History of the Scottish People* (London, 1969) p. 47.
5. This work, produced in three volumes (Edinburgh, 1858-69), is a valuable and enthralling hodge podge of historical information.
6. J. Craigie (ed.), *The Basilicon Doron of King James VI* (Scottish Text Society, Edinburgh, 1944) pp. 82-3.
7. A. Constable (ed.), *A History of Greater Britain . . . by John Major* (S.H.S. Edinburgh, 1892) pp. 30-1.
8. T.C. Smout, 'The landowner and the planned village in Scotland' in N.T. Phillipson and R.M. Mitchison, *Scotland in the Age of Improvement* (Edinburgh, 1970).
9. D. McRoberts, 'The Manse of Stobo in 1542', *Innes Review* vol. XXII (1971).
10. T.Tucker, 'Report upon the settlement of the Revenues of Excise and Custom in Scotland' in *Miscellany of the Scottish Burgh Records Society* (S.B.R.S. Edinburgh, 1881).

11. *Extracts of the Records of the Royal Burgh of Edinburgh* vol. II, 1528-57 (Edinburgh, 1871).
12. *R.P.C.* vol. XIII 1622-5, (Edinburgh, 1846) p.510.
13. W McKày (ed.), *Chronicles of the Frasers* (S.H.S. Edinburgh, 1905) p.207. R. Chambers, *Domestic Annals* vo. I, p.170.

Chapter 2

1. This can be seen by studying the *Fasti* (ed. Hew Scott), 7 vols. (Edinburgh, 1915-28) of the Church of Scotland.
2. Kirk session registers are now gathered together in the SRO.
3. D. Fleming (ed), *Register of the kirk session of St Andrews* vol II, 1582-1600 (S.H.S., Edinburgh, 1890) p. 849.
4. H. Paton (ed.), *The Session Book of Kingarth* (privately published, 1932) p. 200.
5. For Scotland as a whole in the 1850s the percentage of illegitimate births was 8.9, but in some areas, notably the south-west and Banffshire, it was much higher.
6. *Kirk session...St Andrews*, p.922.
7. 'Extracts from the kirk session minutes' in W. Cramond, *The Records of Elgin* vol II (N.S.C. Aberdeen, 1908) p.4.
8. SRO CH 2/377/2.
9. *Kirk Session . . . St Andrews*, p.836.
10. J.M. McPherson, *The Kirk's Care of the Poor* (Aberdeen, n.d.) pp. 25-6.
11. This has been pointed out by Edmund Leach in *Genesis as Myth* (London, 1969).
12. J. Knox, 'The First Blast of the Trumpet against the Monstrous Regiment of Women', 1558, *Works* vol. IV (Edinburgh, 1855).
13. The 1560 Confession is to be found in W.C. Dickinson (ed.) *John Knox's History of the Reformation in Scotland*, vol. II (Edinburgh, 1949), and in John Knox *Works* vol. II.
14. The *Carmina Gadelica* is published in six volumes, (Edinburgh, 1928-69), edited, vols. I-V by A. Carmichael and vol. VI by W. Matheson.
15. These prices are drawn from urban regulations and from figures in G. Donaldson (ed.) *The Thirds of Benefices* (S.H.S. Edinburgh, 1949).
16. See I.H. Stewart, *The Scottish Coinage* (London, 1955) for the weight and quality of sixteenth-century coin.
17. Edited by H. Paton (Edinburgh, 1957).
18. There are some moving reports to the Privy Council in *R.P.C.* vol. XIII (Edinburgh, 1896) pp.815-22.

Chapter 3

1. The main studies are those by G.D. Henderson, in particular *Religious Life in Seventeenth-century Scotland* (Cambridge, 1937).
2. Henderson, *op. cit* p.9.

3. H. Paton (ed.), *The Session Book of Dundonald* (privately published, 1936) pp.462-4.
4. *Reports on the State of Certain Parishes in Scotland, 1627* (M.C. Edinburgh, 1835) p. 22.
5. H. Paton, *Dundonald* pp. 464-8. Payments for pauper children are referred to in G.D. Henderson, *The Scottish Ruling Elder* (London, 1935) p.152.
6. H. Paton (ed.), *The Session Book of Kingarth* (privately published, 1932) pp.18, 25.
7. D. Withrington, 'Lists of Schoolmasters teaching Latin, 1690', *Miscellany X* (S.H.S. Edinburgh, 1965) pp. 119-142.
8. *R.P.C.* Vol XIII (Edinburgh, 1896) p.288, 11 July 1623.
9. *A.P.S.* (Edinburgh, 1870) VII 385 and VIII 89.
10. SRO CH 2/333/2, March 1686.
11. John Nicoll, *A Diary of Public Transactions* (B.C. Edinburgh, 1836) pp. 106, 196, 212, etc.
12. *Chronicles of the Frasers* (S.H.S. Edinburgh, 1905) p. 518. The episode appears to belong to the 1670s.
13. H. Paton (ed.), *The Session Book of Penninghame* (privately published, 1933) vol. I p. 171. Andrew Symson, *A Large Description of Galloway* (Edinburgh, 1823) treats this as the normal form of cleaning up.
14. W. Mackay (ed), *Records of the Presbyteries of Inverness and Dingwall 1643-88.* (S.H.S. Edinburgh, 1896) p. 282.
15. SRO CH 2 337 2, 14 July 1672 and 15 June 1673.
16. The unpublished section of the Register of the Privy Council (SRO typescript) shows this happening in Pittenweem, Fife, 15 February 1705.
17. K. Thomas, *Religion and the Decline of Magic* (London, 1971) pp. 560-9.
18. I owe information of the event to Mrs Frances Burton, late post-graduate student at Edinburgh University, and of the Scandinavian practice to Professor Rolf Seljelid of Tromsø University.
19. R.S. Barclay (ed.), *The Court Book of Orkney and Shetland, 1614-5* (S.H.S. Edinburgh, 1967) pp. 65, 67.
20. P Hume Brown, *Early Travellers in Scotland* (Edinburgh, 1891) pp. 124-8.
21. *Chronicles of the Frasers* p. 245.
22. A. Constable (ed.), *A History of Greater Britain . . . by John Major* (S.H.S. Edinburgh, 1892) p. 48. James Craigie (ed.), *The Basilicon Doron of King James VI* (Edinburgh, 1944) p.71.
23. I.F. Grant, *The Macleods* (London, 1959) p. 246. *The Black Book of Taymouth* (B.C. Edinburgh, 1855) pp. xxvii-xxviii.
24. *Memoir of Sir Ewen Cameron of Lochiel* (Edinburgh, 1842) p. 136.
25. *Chronicles of the Frasers* p.252.
26. *Ibid.* p.333.
27. *Ibid.* pp. 517-8.
28. Martin Martin, *A Description of the Western Isles,* (London, 1703) p. 107.

Chapter 4

1. These instances are from SRO CH 1/2/93, General Assembly papers concerned with a Call to Alloa in 1750.
2. An instance of this can be found in H. Paton (ed.) *The Session Book of Penninghame,* (privately published, 1932) vol. I, p. 114. On this occasion, August 1703, the imminence of the harvest season was used as justification.
3. The inventory is for George Sinclare, SRO CC 8/8/90.
4. SRO CC 22/3/1.
5. *Memoir of Sir Ewen Cameron of Lochiel* (M.C. Edinburgh, 1842) p. 202.
6. SRO GD 18/737 p. 55.
7. This is from the unpublished part of the Register of the Privy Council (SRO typescript) for the date 17 April 1701.
8. Sir John Clerk of Penicuik (the younger) records in his memoir that the building of his fine house at Mavisbank in the 1720s and 1730s relied on the labour of tenants with their carts and horses. J.M. Gray (ed.) *Memoirs of the Life of Sir John Clerk of Penicuik* (S.H.S. Edinburgh, 1892) p. 115.
9. J.G. Fyfe (ed.), *Scottish Diaries and Memoirs,* vol. II (Stirling, 1942) pp. 63-4.
10. SRO GD 18/1200.
11. *North Country Diaries* II (Surtees Society, vol. 124) (Durham, 1915) pp. 32, 39.
12. The calculation has been made by T.H. Hollingsworth using A.J. Coale and P.G. Demeny, *Model Life Tables* (Princeton, 1966).
13. SRO CH 1/2/95.
14. Sir Robert Gordon of Gordonstoun, *The Genealogy of the Earls of Sutherland,* (Edinburgh, 1813) pp. 3-4.
15. W.C. Dickinson, *Two Students at St Andrews, 1711-6* (St Andrews, 1952) p. 17. The early numbers of Scotland's first regular newspaper, the *Edinburgh Courant* from 1705, show that lemons were always on sale in that city. They were probably bought for making punch.
16. J. Colville (ed.) *The Ochtertyre House Book, 1737-9* (S.H.S. Edinburgh, 1909) p. 118.
17. H. Armet (ed.), *Extracts from the Records of the Burgh of Edinburgh, 1689-1701* (Edinburgh, 1962) p.203.
18. The parish diet allowances are from SRO CH 2/407/1, 10 July 1699 for Chirnside, and CH 2/333/2 January 1698 and May 1701 for Spott.
19. M. Goldie, 'The standard of living of rural labourers in selected counties of Scotland as shown in the Old and New Statistical Accounts', Edinburgh M.Sc. thesis, 1971, c.3.
20. New Register House, Parish Register of Kilmarnock.
21. This is repeatedly shewn in the SRO publication *Reports on the Annexed Estates 1755-69* (Edinburgh, 1973).
22. T.C. Smout, 'Goat-keeping in the Old Highland Economy - 4', *S.S.*

vol. IX (1965) p. 187.

23.   Andrew Symson, *A Large Description of Galloway* (Edinburgh, 1823) pp. 116, 119.
24.   This calculation is that made by T.C. Smout in work for the Scottish Historical Demography Unit, Edinburgh University.
25.   SRO CH 2/377/2, 2 August 1969. See also my article on this parish in the *Transactions of the East Lothian Antiquarian Society* vol. XIV (1975).

Chapter 5

1.   A.R.B. Haldane, *Three Centuries of Scottish Posts* (Edinburgh, 1971) p. 305.
2.   J.P.S. Ferguson, *Scottish Newspapers held in Scottish Libraries* (Scottish Central Library, 1956).
3.   See above, chapter 4, Page 64.
4.   I.F. Grant, *Everyday Life on an old Highland Farm* (London, 1924) p. 272.
5.   These materials became known to, if not used by, many ranks of society. The reference in a Galloway inventory of 1750 to 'McHogginie' show a readiness to assimilate new commodities to local society. Inventory of Thomas Kennedy, SRO CC 22/3/2.
6.   G. Loch, *The Family of Loch* (Edinburgh, 1934) p. 177.
7.   G. Menary, *Life and Letters of Duncan Forbes of Culloden*, (London, 1936) pp.144-9.
8.   SRO CC 8/8/104.
9.   G. Goudie (ed.), *Diary of the Reverend John Mill* (S.H.S. Edinburgh, 1889) p.17.
10.   Adam Petrie, *Rules of Good Deportment* (republished Edinburgh, 1835) p.86.
11.   E. Cregeen, 'The Tacksmen and their Successors', *S.S.* XIII (1969) pp. 93-114. *Reports on the Annexed Estates, 1755-69*, (Edinburgh, 1973) pp. 11, 17-18.
12.   The *Scots Courant*, November 1711, carries the advertisements of the nursery garden of Samuel Robertson at Kelso, who had thorns for hedging; in 1722 there was also a nursery at Tyninghame advertising fruit trees.
13.   J.M. Gray (ed), *Memoirs of the Life of Sir John Clerk of Penicuik* (S.H.S. Edinburgh, 1892) pp. 18, 20.
14.   J. Colville (ed.) *Letters of John Cockburn of Ormistoun to his Gardener* (S.H.S. Edinburgh, 1914) p. 25. These criticisms of the quality of fresh vegetables in the capital have some validity still in the later twentieth century.
15.   F.A. Pottle (ed.), *Boswell's London Journal 1762-3*, (London, 1950) p.26.
16.   R. Scott-Moncrieff (ed.), *The Household Book of Lady Grisell Baillie, 1692-1737* (S.H.S. Edinburgh, 1911) pp. 155-6, 276.
17.   T. Bewick, *Memoir* (London, 1862) p. 99.
18.   Introduction to the Lothians volume of the new edition of the *O.S.A.*

19. See above, chapter 4 p. 68.
20. 1829 edition, p. 111.
21. SRO CH 1/2/85, 86 and 87.
22. J. Thomson, *General View of the Agriculture of the County of Fife...* (Edinburgh, 1800) p. 29.
23. Thirlage was the obligation on a tenant to get his corn ground at a particular mill. Where land, or mills, had changed hands it could become entwined very deeply in property rights.
24. MSS of the Sinclairs of Ulbster at Thurso East Mains, vol. II p. 273, 10 April 1802, Dempster to Sir John Sinclair.
25. E. Smith, *Memoirs of a Highland Lady* (London, 1898) p. 162.
26. I.F. Grant, *op. cit* c. 7 and Appendix I.
27. SRO GD 18/1217.
28. A.J. Durie, 'The Scottish Linen Industry, 1707-75, with particular reference to the early history of the British Linen Company', Edinburgh Ph. D thesis, 1972, p. 77.
29. A good example of this is the catechising list made by the minister of South Leith 1740-55, SRO CH 2/716/327.
30. Typescript of the Acts of the Privy Council, SRO. SRO CH 2/357/19.
31. H. Paton (ed.) *The Session Book of Penninghame* (privately published, 1933) vol. II pp. 198-9. The session had, in fact, prosecuted a couple for asserting that embezzlement was taking place, 20 years earlier, when the same treasurer was in office, vol. I p. 267.
32. W.H. Morison, *Dictionary of Decisions...* vol. XXV-VI, P. 10555, and SRO CH 2/389/4.
33. Historical Manuscripts Commission, *Report on...the manuscripts of . . . Lord Polwarth*, vol. V (London, 1961) p. 146.
34. *Reports on the Annexed Estates, 1755-69* (Edinburgh, 1973) p.23.
35. E.g. by Lord Grange in Mar and Kellie Papers, SRO GD 124/15/1262 and 1264.
36. *Caledonian Mercury* 4 January 1772 shows that Glasgow was adopting, and Edinburgh already had, a subscription system for prosecuting thieves.
37. E. Richards, 'How Tame were the Highlanders during the Clearances?' *S.S.* vol. XVII, (1973) pp. 35-50.
38. I.G. Lindsay and M.Cosh, *Inveraray and the Dukes of Argyll* (Edinburgh, 1973) p. 34.
39. A. McPherson, 'An Old Highland Parish Register' ii *S.S.* vol XII (1968) pp. 81-111.
40. Lindsay and Cosh, *op. cit.* pp. 271-6.
41. E. Cregeen (ed.), *Argyll Estate Instructions; Mull, Morvern, Tiree, 1771-1805,* (S.H.S. Edinburgh, 1964) pp. xvii-xxxv.
42. J. Colville, *op. cit.* p. 18.
43. Black's *Picturesque Tourist of Scotland* (Edinburgh, 1865) p. 468. Similar comments can be found in W.O. Jarratt, *Reminiscences of a Tour in Scotland* (Driffield, 1854).

44. John Murray, *Handbook for Travellers in Scotland* (London, 1867) p. xlii.
45. *Reports on the Annexed Estates* (Edinburgh, 1973) p. 35.

Chapter 6

1. Adam Smith, *The Wealth of Nations* (ed. E. Cannan; London, 1961) vol. I, p. 8.
2. *O.S.A.* vol. VII, p. 88.
3. A. Brown, *History of Glasgow*, (Glasgow, 1795-7) vol. II, pp. 240-4.
   E. Baines, *History of the Cotton Manufacture of Great Britain*, (London, 1835) p. 390. L.J. Saunders, *Scottish Democracy* (Edinburgh, 1950) p. 103.
4. The story can be found in greater detail in T.C. Smout, *History of the Scottish People* (London, 1969) p. 25 ff.
5. *My Schools and Schoolmasters* (Edinburgh, 1858) p. 317.
6. *P.P.* 1842, XV pp. 29, 93, 103.
7. *O.S.A.* vol. XIII p. 165, from 3d a day with food to one shilling a day and food, and also vol. VI p. 160. V. Morgan, 'Agricultural Wage Rates in late eighteenth-century Scotland', *Economic History Review* 2nd series, vol. XXIV, 1971.
8. *Autobiography of a Working Man* (London, 1855) p.2.
9. For instance Duns. See W. Morison, *Dictionary of Decisions* (Edinburgh, 1811) p. 10591, Pollock vs Darling, 1804.
10. *Autobiography*, p.4. I am informed by Mrs Ailsa Maxwell that the grudge was unfounded: his name is in the register.
11. M. Goldie, 'The Standard of Living of the Scottish Farm Labourer in selected areas at the time of the two Statistical Accounts', Edinburgh M.Sc. thesis, 1970, c.3. M. Flinn, 'Trends in real wages', *Economic History Review* 2nd series, vol. XXVII, 1974, p. 407.
12. These are *P.P.* 1831-2 XV and *P.P.* 1833 XXI.
13. *P.P.* 1831-2 XV p. 352. This gives an interesting glimpse of an accepted working-class dinner.
14. These can be found for Edinburgh, for instance, in the *Scots Magazine*, which started in 1743.
15. J. Stark, 'Contributions to the vital Statistics of Scotland', *Journal of the Royal Statistical Society*, vol. XIV, 1851, p. 85.
16. *P.P.* 1833 XXI pp. 13 and 42.
17. *Scotsman* 13 January 1838.
18. N. Gash, *Sir Robert Peel* (London, 1972) p. 441.
19. *P.P.* 1844 XXII, p. 727 (The Report of the Royal Commission on the Relief of Poverty in Scotland).
20. Scotland's preference in urban buildings for the tall tenement is often attributed to her feudal land law. But it is worth noting that the same type of building obtains even in towns where the housing was built directly by the feudal superior. See I.G. Lindsay and M. Cosh, *Inveraray and the Dukes of Argyll* (Edinburgh, 1973).
21. E. Chadwick, *Report on the Sanitary Condition of the Labouring Population*

of Great Britain. ed. M.W. Flinn, (Edinburgh, 1965) p.119. Even this ruthless report was, in typical nineteenth-century fashion, not prepared to use explicit words about human excrement.

22. The area taken as Highland is that defined as such in F. Fraser Darling, *West Highland Survey* (Oxford, 1955) pp. 15-17, and the figures come from p. 76 of this useful book.

23. *Statistics of the Annexed Estates* (Edinburgh, 1973). For comparison see M. Gray, *The Highland Economy, 1750-1850* (Edinburgh, 1957) pp. 24, 138, 198 for later figures.

24. *Journal* (Edinburgh, 1874) vol.II p. 248.

25. P.G Askell, *Morvern Transformed* (Cambridge, 1968) p. 27 and elsewhere shows that clearances carried out by a landowner living in a traditional manner on his estates caused much less resentment than those of incoming or remote people.

26. R. Adam (ed.), *Sutherland Estate Papers* (S.H.S. Edinburgh, 1972) vol. II p. 194. The event was in 1813.

27. R.N. McMichael, 'The Potato Famine of the 1840s in the Western Highlands and Islands of Scotland', Edinburgh University M.A. thesis, 1973, Economic History Department, p. 16.

Chapter 7

1. Hugh Miller, *My Schools and Schoolmasters* (Edinburgh, 1856) p. 178.
2. *P.P.* 1844 XVI p. 10.
3. *P.P.* 1837-8 VIII p. 75.
4. *P.P.* 1830 XXII p. 189.
5. Miller, *op. cit* p. 151.
6. N. Smelser, *Social Change in the Industrial Revolution* (London, 1959) pp. 186-96.
7. *Scotsman* 13 January 1838.
8. W. Tait, *Magdelanism* (Edinburgh, 1840).
9. L.K. Haldane, *Friends and Kindred* (London, 1961) pp. 73-4.
10. T. Pinney (ed.). *The Letters of Thomas Babington Macaulay* (Cambridge, 1974) p. 241.
11. W.O. Jarratt, *Reminiscences of a Tour in Scotland* (Driffield, 1854) p. 121.
12. *P.P.* 1847 XIII p. 133.
13. SRO CH 1/2, The Papers of the general assembly. In about a quarter of the Calls women were listed as heads of households.
14. Miller, *Op. cit* p. 183.
15. *O.S.A.* VII p. 338.
16. T.J. Howell, continuation of W. Cobbett, *State Trials* vol XXIII (London, 1817) column 215.
17. *N.S.A.* III part 3, p. 27.
18. *N.S.A.* I p. 543.
19. *P.P.* 1837-8 VIII p.22, evidence of C. Todd.
20. *Ibid.* p. 49, evidence of Angus Campbell.

21. *Ibid.* pp. 58, 69, 70, evidence of James McNish.
22. *Ibid.* pp. 97, 147.
23. *P.P.* 1870 XI pp. 74, 287, evidence of F.J. Cochran and W.S. Walker.
24. *P.P.* 1837-8, XXI p.6.
25. *P.P.* 1837-8, VIII pp. 164-7.
26. *P.P.* 1844 XVI p. 36.
27. David Buchan, *The Ballad and the Folk* (London, 1972) chapters 13-15.
28. Ian Carter, 'Class and Culture among Farm Servants in the North-east, 1840-1914' in A. A. MacLaren (ed.) *Social Class in Scotland* (Edinburgh, 1976.)
29. M.Gray, 'Scottish Emigration: the Social Impact of Agrarian Change in the Rural Lowlands 1775-1875', *Perspectives in American History* VII (1973) is an illuminating study of the effects of various agricultural patterns on the structure of rural society. D. Toulmin, *Hard Shining Corn* (Aberdeen, 1972) is a collection of stories which shows the unity of northern rural society.
30. I. Donnachie, 'Orbiston: A Scottish Owenite Community, 1825-8' in J. Butt (ed.) *Robert Owen, Prince of Cotton Spinners* (Newton Abbot, 1971) pp. 135-67.
31. Alexander Wilson, *The Chartist Movement in Scotland* (Manchester, 1970) p. 183.
32. *P.P.* 1847 XIII, Report of the Select Committee on sites for churches in Scotland, *passim*. Thomas Guthrie described preaching at Canonbie in February 1844: 'When my hat was off during the last prayer, some man kindly extended an umbrella over my head', 1st report, p. 72.
33. *Ibid.* p. 16.
34. A.A. MacLaren, *Religion and Social Class* (London, 1974) p. 55.
35. *P.P.* 1840 XXVI, 5th report on Prisons of Scotland, pp. viii-ix.
36. R.A. Cage and E.O.A. Checkland, 'Thomas Chalmers and Urban Poverty: the St John's Parish Experiment in Glasgow, 1819-1837.' *Philosophical Journal* vol XIII (1976).
37. R.N. McMichael, 'The potato famine of the 1840s in the Western Highlands and Islands of Scotland', Edinburgh University M.A. thesis. Department of Economic History, 1973.
38. *P.P.* 1870 XI, Report of the Select Committee on the operation of the Poor Law in Scotland, pp. 127-9, evidence of James Moir. *P.P.* 1868-9, *Ibid.*, p. 177-8, evidence of A.H. McLellan and A. McLaren.
39. *P.P.* 1870 XI, p. 118, evidence of A. Grey.
40. This information, with much else on the new poor law, comes from conversation with Dr Audrey Paterson of Edinburgh University.
41. G.S. Pryde, *Central and Local Government in Scotland since 1707*, Historical Association Pamphlet G.45, (London, 1960) p. 15.
42. *P.P.* 1840 XXVI p. iv; *P.P.* 1836 XXXV p. 15.
43. H. Cockburn, *Circuit Journeys* (Edinburgh, 1889) p. 17.
44. e.g. *P.P.* 1840 XXVI p. 22: see also U.H.R. Henriques, 'The Rise of the Separate System of Prison Discipline', *Past and Present* 54 (1972) pp. 61-93.

45. Verbal communication by D. Paton, late research student, Department of Economic History, Edinburgh University.

Chapter 8

1.   F.G. Rea, *A School in South Uist*, (London, 1964).
2.   A. Drummond and J. Bullough, *The Church in Victorian Scotland* (Edinburgh, 1975) c.1 and 2.
3.   H. Wylie, 'Religion and the Working Class in Scotland, 1870-1914' Edinburgh University M.A. thesis, 1976, Department of Economic History.
4.   Drummond and Bullough, *op. cit.* p. 322.
5.   P.C. Simpson, *The Life of Principal Rainy* (London, 1909) p. 441.
6.   J.S. Black and G. Chrystal, *The Life of William Robertson Smith* (London, 1912) p. 431.
7.   *P.P.* 1884 XXXII, The Report of the Royal Commission into the Crofters and Cottars in the Highlands and Islands of Scotland, (The Napier Commission) p.85.
8.   P. Gaskell, *Morvern Transformed* (Cambridge, 1968).
9.   E. Muir, *An Autobiography* (London, 1954)
10. M.W. Flinn (ed.), *Scottish Population History from the seventeenth century to the 1930s* (Cambridge, 1977) Part V.
11. Napier Commission, evidence. *P.P.* 1884 XXXIV p. 1011.
12. M.Gray, 'Scottish Emigration: the Social Impact of Agrarian Change in the Rural Lowlands, 1775-1875'. *Perspectives in American History* vol VII (1973).
13. *P.P.* 1893-4 XXXVI pp. 243, 306, 394, 467. The Royal Commission on Labour. The Agricultural Labourer, Scotland.
14. Lavinia Derwent, *A Breath of Border Air* (London, 1975) p. 13.
15. J. Stark, 'Replies to Queries as to the Treatment of Infants', *Journal of the Royal Statistical Society* vol XXIX (1866).
16. A. Slaven, *The Development of the West of Scotland 1750-1960* (London, 1975) p. 256.
17. *P.P.* 1917-8 XIV, Report of the Royal Commission on the Housing of the Industrial Population in Scotland.
18. A.K. Chalmers, *The Health of Glasgow* (Glasgow, 1930) pp. 314, 330, 343.
19. *P.P.* 1884-5, XXXI p.69. Second Report of the Royal Commission on the Housing of the Working Class.
20. D.N. Paton, J.C. Dunlop and E. Inglis, *A Study of the Diet of the Labouring Classes in Edinburgh* (Edinburgh, 1902) pp. 17,18.
21. Slaven, *op. cit* p. 148.
22. T.C. Smout, 'Aspects of Sexual Behaviour in Nineteenth-Century Scotland', in A.A. MacLaren (ed.) *Social Class in Scotland* (Edinburgh, 1976).
23. *P.P.* 1895 XVII p. 535. Report of the Royal Commission on Agriculture, Assistant Commissioner's report.
24. T.C. Smout, *op, cit.*

Index

Dairsie 84
Deanston 98
Dempster, George, of Dunnichen 85
Depopulation 149
Diarrhoea 69, 154
Diet 65, 70-2, 82, 103, 104, 152, 155-6, 173
Dingwall 51
Disease 89, 107-8, 154
  see also Dysentery, Fever, Plague,
    Smallpox, Turberculosis, Typhoid,
    Typhus
Disestablishment 161
Disruption of the Church 129-33, 145
Dissent 63, 87, 130
  see also Church, Episcopalian and
    Church, Free
Doctors 138-9, 158
Dornoch 148
Drink 31, 55, 87, 170
  see also Beer, Drunkenness, Tea, Whisky
Drumdelgie 115, 127-8
Drunkenness 87, 137, 155, 160-1
Dunbar, William 11
Dundee 101, 105-6, 153, 155, 156, 157,
  160
Dundonald 43, 44-5
Dunfermline 23
Dunstaffnage 65
Dunvegan 57
Dysentery 69, 108

East Lothian 24, 29, 36, 44
  see also Lothians
Edinburgh 22, 23, 50, 63, 66-67, 79, 91,
  109
  in the nineteenth century 121-2, 155
  housing in 155
  industries in 101
  poor relief in 88, 135-6
  prostitution in 119
Edinburgh Courant 76, 170
Education 41, 43-6, 91, 136-8, 143, 151,
  158-9, 165
Education Act (1872) 143, 150-1, 158
Educational Institute of Scotland 138
Elgin 12, 32
Emigration 36, 102, 110, 142
Erskine, Reverend Ebenezer 130
Eskdale 123
Evangelicalism 130

Factories 96-8, 101, 103-4
Fala and Soutra 125
Famine 48-9, 71, 89, 94, 135
Feu-farm 17
Feudalism 15-6, 91
Feudal jurisdictions 91

Fever 69, 108
Fife 23, 84, 87
Fishing 109, 112, 147, 149
Food shortage 36, 70-4, 82, 88-9, 94, 102,
  112
  see also Famine
Forbes, Duncan 77
Forfeited estates commission 91, 94
Forks 78-9
Forres 136
Fort William *see* Inverlochy
Fostering 59
Fraser chronicle *see* Wardlaw chronicle
Frasers 55, 59-60
French, use of 13
Frendraught, feud of 55
Fuel 85
  see also Coal industry
Fundamentalism 145
Furniture 42, 64-5, 96, 171

Gaelic 13, 93, 143, 150-1
Galashiels 125
Galloway 64-5, 72, 169, 171
General Assembly 28, 67, 78-80, 119,
  131, 145-6
Germany 36
Glasgow 87, 91, 99, 101, 125-6, 138
  crime in 160
  housing in 108, 154-6
  poor relief in 134, 135
Glass 23, 68, 102
Glenorchy, Campbells of 58, 59
Golf 148
Gordon, Sir John, of Gordonstoun 70
Gordons 54-5, 58
Grant, Elizabeth, of Rothiemurchus 85
Grants 59
Great Rebellion 40
Greenock 108, 154

Haldane, Kathleen 121
Hardie, Keir 162, 163-4
Heritors 62, 87-90
  see also lairds
Highlands
  before 1800 13-14, 51, 55-60, 72, 90-4
  after 1800 109, 110-13, 147-51, 165
  poor relief in 135
  population in 90, 109-111
Hinds 85, 107
  see also Labourers
Homes 14
Housing 42, 121, 165
  rural 66, 67-9, 84, 94, 102, 149, 152
  urban 108, 153-5, 173
Humbie 101